GW00374926

Rethinking Interdisciplinarity across the
Social Sciences and Neurosciences

DOI: 10.1057/9781137407962.0001

Other Palgrave Pivot titles

DOI: 10.1057/9781137407962.000

palgrave▸pivot

Rethinking Interdisciplinarity across the Social Sciences and Neurosciences

▶ Felicity Callard
Reader in Social Science for Medical Humanities, Durham University, UK

and

Des Fitzgerald
Lecturer in Sociology, Cardiff University, UK

palgrave
macmillan

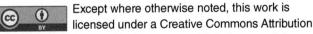
DOI: 10.1057/9781137407962.0001

First published 2015 by
PALGRAVE MACMILLAN

Palgrave Macmillan in the UK is an imprint of Macmillan Publishers Limited, registered in England, company number 785998, of Houndmills, Basingstoke, Hampshire RG21 6XS.

Palgrave Macmillan in the US is a division of St Martin's Press LLC, 175 Fifth Avenue, New York, NY 10010.

Palgrave Macmillan is the global academic imprint of the above companies and has companies and representatives throughout the world.

Palgrave® and Macmillan® are registered trademarks in the United States, the United Kingdom, Europe and other countries.

ISBN: 978–1–137–40797–9 EPUB
ISBN: 978–1–137–40796–2 PDF
ISBN: 978–1–137–40795–5 Hardback

A catalogue record for this book is available from the British Library.

A catalog record for this book is available from the Library of Congress.

www.palgrave.com/pivot

DOI: 10.1057/9781137407962

▶ *To Jan & John Callard*
To Bridie Connaughton

DOI: 10.1057/9781137407962.0001

Contents

DOI: 10.1057/9781137407962.0001

DOI: 10.1057/9781137407962.0001

Acknowledgements

We acknowledge many collaborators, co-authors and interlocutors with whom we have worked and thought and discussed and argued over many years, as we have traversed the interdisciplinary spaces that we discuss here. This book could not – we are deadly serious – have been written without them. We thank Ben Alderson-Day, Josh Berson, Thomas Brunotte, Suparna Choudhury, Charles Fernyhough, Giovanni Frazzetto, Philipp Haueis, Russ Hurlburt, Nev Jones, Simone Kühn, Ruth Leys, Melissa Littlefield, Simon Lovestone, Jane Macnaughton, Daniel Margulies, Harriet Martin, Dan O'Connor, Constantina Papoulias, Holly Pester, Eugene Raikhel, Mary Robson, Andreas Roepstorff, Diana Rose, Nikolas Rose, Ilina Singh, Jan Slaby, Jonny Smallwood, Kimberley Staines, Will Viney, Scott Vrecko, Pat Waugh, James Wilkes, Angela Woods, Til Wykes, and Allan Young. We draw, occasionally, here on arguments, data and material that we have developed, in published and unpublished work and conference presentations, with some of those mentioned above; we are grateful for their generosity in allowing us to use (and abuse) these materials.

We are enormously grateful to the funders who have supported interdisciplinary research across the social sciences, neurosciences and humanities, and whose workshops and grant schemes have been pivotal to the research that underpins this book. The Wellcome Trust, via its award to Hubbub to become the first residency of The Hub at Wellcome Collection, has been an extraordinary funder and interlocutor, and has been

DOI: 10.1057/9781137407962.0001

indispensable to our and to many of our collaborators' endeavours to think through and produce interdisciplinary research. We also thank the Volkswagen Foundation (which funded our interdisciplinary workshop on Experimental Entanglements in Cognitive Neuroscience; as well as the grant 'Wandering Minds: Interdisciplinary Experiments on Self-Generated Thought'); the European Science Foundation (via the European Neuroscience and Society Network, which funded both of us to attend a 'Neuroschool'); the Economic and Social Research Council (via a Transforming Social Science award on mental life and the metropolis); the National Institute for Health Research (via the award to the specialist Biomedical Research Centre for Mental Health (South London & Maudsley Foundation Trust and Institute of Psychiatry, Psychology & Neuroscience, King's College London)), where Felicity was based for several years; and The Wellcome Trust (again!) for its Strategic Award to the Centre for Medical Humanities and Strategic Award to Hearing the Voice – two other interdisciplinary projects that have been central to the work we reflect on here.

We thank the various academic centres, departments and institutions that have supported and enabled our interdisciplinary research and thinking: the Centre for Medical Humanities and Department of Geography, Durham University; the BIOS Centre, London School of Economics; King's College London (both the Department of Social Science, Health & Medicine and the Institute of Psychiatry, Psychology & Neuroscience); the Max Planck Institute for the History of Science, Berlin; and the Interacting Minds Centre, Aarhus University.

We are hugely grateful for the imagination and generosity of Nicola Jones, Sharla Plant, and all of their colleagues at Palgrave Macmillan, for everything that they have done to support this volume right the way through. What started as a vague urge, some years ago, to torque the conversation on interdisciplinarity in a particular way, would not have been possible without their openness, and patience, as the final form of the book took shape. We could not have wished for a better publishing team.

We are particularly grateful to Charles Fernyhough, Daniel Margulies, Constantina Papoulias, Nikolas Rose, James Wilkes, and Angela Woods, who read drafts of the book in its entirety. Their astute comments, critiques and, at times, significant disagreements with our interpretations and analyses, were indispensable as we were revising the volume. To a very significant extent, they enabled us to bring this volume into the world.

DOI: 10.1057/9781137407962.0002

While the work that we discuss in this book draws extensively on the insights and expertise of many of the people and organizations that we enumerate above, we stress that the two of us, alone, are responsible for the entirety of the contents of the book.

This work was supported by The Wellcome Trust [103817/Z/14/Z], which also enabled this book to be published Open Access.

DOI: 10.1057/9781137407962.0002

OPEN

Introduction: Not Another Book about Interdisciplinarity

Abstract: *In the introduction, we introduce our monograph, Rethinking Interdisciplinarity, as a report from the interdisciplinary field – and an account of our own attempts to work and live across the social sciences and neurosciences. The introduction sets out the core goal of the volume, which is to give a sense, beyond bland encouragements, of what actually goes into, and what goes on in, interdisciplinary projects. The introduction sets out the core reasons that we have pursued interdisciplinary research, with our collaborators, across the neurosciences and social sciences – but it also establishes our view that interdisciplinarity is nonetheless a problem, or a set of problems, to be analysed in its own right.*

Keywords: entanglement; interdisciplinarity; neuroscience; social science

Callard, Felicity and Des Fitzgerald. *Rethinking Interdisciplinarity across the Social Sciences and Neurosciences.* Basingstoke: Palgrave Macmillan, 2015. DOI: 10.1057/9781137407962.0003.

A few years ago, we were at an interdisciplinary workshop for researchers who were broadly interested in the intersections between the neurosciences, the humanities, and the social sciences. We had arrived, separately, at the workshop, as two social scientists (FC as a cultural and health geographer; DF as a sociologist) who had been working on projects that were more-or-less *about* some aspect of the neurosciences, psychology, or psychiatry – but who had also lately begun to suspect, quite independently of one another, that we might be able to make more interesting interventions by somehow collaborating *with* people in those sciences, rather than simply scrutinizing them, from the outside, as objects of historical, cultural, or sociological attention. We didn't know one another at that point, and we found ourselves on the margins of the same group – where we fell into conversation about how we had come to be engaged with the life sciences, about our hopes for the meeting, and about our anxieties and excitement *vis-à-vis* actually doing something more experimentally interdisciplinary. Central to our conversation was a shared sense that the conventional theoretical assumptions and methodological manoeuvres that we had each inherited from our own discipline (geography and sociology, respectively), and which were supposed to help us understand the biosciences, were, in fact, quite inadequate to a moment in which those same sciences seemed ever more richly and capaciously *social* in both their orientation and their practice.

And so there we were, feeling somewhat at sea both socially and epistemologically, when one of the organizers of the meeting approached us, asking whether we were having a good conversation, and whether we could see any interdisciplinary opportunities. *Uh, yes, we could! There were certainly all sorts of crossovers between our different geographical and sociological inheritances; we were sure that there were various ways in which we might develop an interdisciplinary collaboration.* All seemed well. But then it became clear that we had not yet hooked up with any neuroscientists. We had thought, then, that because the two of us were from two distinct disciplines, that our incipient collaboration would already count as 'interdisciplinary'. But it appeared that it was a bit of a problem: we were not, as it turned out, having an interdisciplinary conversation with one another at all. In fact, what 'interdisciplinarity' meant in this space, despite some loose talk, was actually something quite specific – and this specific thing did not include the coming together of a geographer and a sociologist. It essentially meant a neuroscientist plus some others. The implicit address to all those of us (philosophers, bioethicists, lawyers,

DOI: 10.1057/9781137407962.0003

psychologists, social scientists) in the room who were not neuroscientists was: find yourself a neuroscientist; design an experiment together; allow your own expertise to nuance some conceptual part of the design; and then get out of the way. This, it became increasingly clear as the workshop moved into its second, and then its third day, was the model of interdisciplinarity on offer.

Well, the two of us did, eventually, find a neuroscientist – and we ended up working together on methodological and substantive issues of interest to each of us. And so, maybe the organizer was right in adjudicating how best to orient people towards putting together collaborative projects. Still, and albeit only in retrospect, this was an early clue that there was a lot more going on beneath the surface of these interdisciplinary attempts to bring together neuroscientists, social scientists, and humanities scholars than either of us had imagined. In fact, beneath the frictionless imaginary of equably co-labouring humanities scholars, scientists, and social scientists – each with her own, dedicated tasks to perform – heterogeneous organizations, individuals, and technologies were creating a very specific, and surprisingly powerful, intellectual space. This space, moreover, for all the talk about its openness and creativity, had some sharp edges – as well as what we increasingly came to identify as surprisingly conservative inheritances. Over the years that followed that workshop, we continued to work across the social sciences and neurosciences, separately and together, and usually with others too. This was not, at least initially, because we were interested in 'interdisciplinarity' in its own right. Rather, we were convinced, as many others have been before us (e.g. Rose 2013), that one could no longer talk about human social life, in all its complexity, contest, history, and nuance, as if that life were not *also* threaded through the biological propensities of an assemblage of human animals (as well as non-human animals, and indeed non-humans in general). And *vice versa*: that new, sophisticated, and nuanced tools for taking – and analysing – biological measures (it was measures of brain function that especially captured our attention) needed to be situated within thicker, more capacious attention to the 'social' than was then on offer.

We came to believe, as we pursued this intuition, that the increasingly formalized space of 'interdisciplinarity' between the life sciences, the social sciences, and the humanities, which we saw being assembled, was not necessarily a boon to attempts to think the 'bio' and the 'social' together. This space of interdisciplinary research on the mind and

DOI: 10.1057/9781137407962.0003

brain was becoming, in fact, a significant problem in its own right. This volume is our attempt to think about that problem. We are interested, here, not so much in providing a theoretical analysis (we have done this elsewhere; see e.g. Fitzgerald and Callard 2015), nor in providing a history of the numerous efforts to create interdisciplinary domains or disciplines within and across the sciences, social sciences, and humanities (see e.g. Graff 2015). Instead, we treat the emergence of this space – the space of 'interdisciplinarity' as it engages the neurosciences, social sciences, and humanities – as a historical and sociological artefact, an object that offers numerous openings as well as constraints. Working through our own memories, reflections, and feelings from the last five years or so, we ask: What is this space? What forms of practice and ethics does it call us towards? What holds it together? What have its various analysts not told us? How does it end up deadening and closing down possibilities, even as it abounds in affirmations of its innovativeness and creativity? And how, if it really is as problematic as we think it is, might it be reimagined and practised differently? What, we ask, would a delicate, difficult, transgressive, risky, playful, and genuinely *experimental* interdisciplinarity involving neuroscientists, social scientists, and humanities scholars actually look like? And what, moreover, might it be able to achieve?

Interdisciplinarity is a term that everyone invokes and none understands. We have lost track of the number of articles, broadsides, reports, and monographs that we have read that have variously defined, championed, dissected, and excoriated interdisciplinarity. 'Interdisciplinarity has come to be', Andrew Barry and Georgina Born rightly note, in an unusually substantial analysis of the logics of interdisciplinarity, 'at once a governmental demand, a reflexive orientation within the academy and an object of knowledge' (Barry and Born 2013, 4). What follows springs from our deep dissatisfaction with much of what passes as 'interdisciplinarity' – both in theory and practice. Its arguments are built from our immersion, over many years, in reading, writing about, and practising many forms of interdisciplinary research. Along the way, we have become increasingly irritated with the normative weight that that this prefix – inter- – has come to carry. A kind of transgression is apparently achieved by working *between* one discipline and another – and yet fundamental assumptions (e.g. about what an experiment might be, about who does it, about how its objects are produced, and so on) are left quite unquestioned. We have been repeatedly struck by how profoundly

DOI: 10.1057/9781137407962.0009

uninteresting – and how conservative – much self-described interdisciplinary scholarship and practice actually is.

We are committed to the view that the particular arena with which we're concerned deserves better than much of the 'interdisciplinary' research that has taken place around it. That arena comprises minds, brains, bodies – as well as, crucially, their relations with what the neurologist and psychiatrist Kurt Goldstein described as an organism's *milieu* (namely, 'that part [of the world] that is adequate to it, that is, that allows for the described relationship between the organism and its environment' (Goldstein 1995 [1934], 106)). There have been a number of overtures from 'the neurosciences' *vis-à-vis* the need to engage with 'the social sciences' – and, simultaneously, many social scientists and humanities scholars who have engaged with neuroscientists. But there are strikingly few examples of research involving both neuroscientists and social scientists that have managed to avoid simply acceding to the epistemological and methodological demands of one half of the dyad. And this 'interdisciplinary science' is not going to disappear any time soon. So there are potent intellectual and practical reasons that underpin the arguments we make for new ways of thinking about and undertaking interdisciplinary research.

At the same time, we – in collaboration with many others – have, for a number of years, struggled to develop modes of thinking and practice that do something slightly different in that same space, without obviating the inequalities (see Chapter 6) and complex emotional demands (see Chapter 7) that characterize the terrain on which interdisciplinary social scientific and neuroscientific research takes place. Our book is also an attempt to make sense of those efforts for a broader audience: we want to present, for wider discussion, some of those modes of collaborative thinking and practice. And we want to be honest, for once, about what interdisciplinarity actually looks and feels like – certainly in terms of the often challenging day-to-day realities that people from all disciplinary backgrounds experience when they live 'between' disciplines, but also in terms of the modes and practices through which we, in collaboration with others from other disciplines, have been able to open up some interesting research directions and problems that address the 'bio' and the 'social' simultaneously (see Chapters 2 and 4). We hope that we might pique others' curiosity, and even widen their potential repertoires, either as they enter this terrain for the first time, or as they persist with long-standing interdisciplinary collaborations.

DOI: 10.1057/9781137407962.0003

We remain convinced that there are many more research questions in this problem-space to be burrowed into, and opened up. This is important not only for reasons of intrinsic interest, but because this terrain – comprising minds, brains, and their environments – encompasses many of the most pressing societal questions of our age. These include, but are not limited to: how to attend to mental distress and psychopathology as phenomena that bring the neurological, psychological, psychopharmacological, and sociological together in deeply complex ways; how to understand the ways in which particular social phenomena and social relations (such as poverty, urban living, familial dynamics, migratory patterns) are entangled with physiological and neurological differences; and how to unpick, and expand, the dense histories and debates that are built into the neurobiological and psychological models through which many people today understand themselves – through which, indeed, they have come to be understood. We add the proviso that much of the book focuses more on how to conceptualize some of these problems, and how to design and analyse the means through which collaborative research across the social sciences and the neurosciences might best tackle them, than on reporting extensive outcomes of interdisciplinary research that we have (already) completed to advance those particular research areas. The book is, in many ways, a 'report from the field'.

The modes of thinking and working that we consider in this volume have been strongly inflected by particular arrangements of institutions, funders, and cross-disciplinary debates. We are able to discuss, analyse, critique, and propose various configurations in this volume only because of the prior and contemporaneous labours of a significant number of individuals who have, for many years, been tinkering with, advocating, and bringing into being opportunities for collaboration across the mind and brain sciences. While this book does not present a history of interdisciplinary collaborations in this arena, we are very aware of the pioneers and fellow travellers whose endeavours have, to a significant extent, underpinned our own enquiries, and we provide some additional details about these people, organizations, and funders in Chapter 1. Together, these have characterized the space of early twenty-first century 'interdisciplinary' research about the mind and brain. And so we also understand this volume as a set of reflections that will – in time – perhaps become part of the archive of a specific moment in the history of the human sciences.

DOI: 10.1057/9781137407962.0009

Experimental entanglements

Some of you might well have been told, as we both have been variously told, by your mentors, supervisors, university, or research institute, that interdisciplinarity is the future. If you have received that message, it might well have generated a variety of emotions in you, and we are certainly not assuming that all of them will have been positive. But if everyone seems to be talking about interdisciplinarity, it's far from clear how many are actually doing it, and, if so, to what effect. Accounts of what interdisciplinary projects are like *in practice* are still relatively few in number, and most people are still reticent about the quotidian experiences that characterize them. There are especially few accounts of occasions in which social scientists and humanities scholars have been experimenters alongside scientists (though see Lane et al. 2011 for an account of an experiment in which knowledge regarding flooding was co-produced across these domains; see also Rabinow and Bennett 2012).

Of course, the neurosciences are themselves already a profoundly interdisciplinary endeavour (which brings together biology, chemistry, physics, cognitive science, computer science, engineering, mathematics, neurology, genetics, and psychology) (Adelman 2010; Rose and Abi-Rached 2013). When one refers, then, to a neuroscientist, one might be referring to someone with a background in physics or mathematics or psychology or philosophy (to name just a few). When we talk about the neurosciences in this volume, we are largely referring to cognitive neuroscience (i.e. the field that addresses the relationship between mental/cognitive functions and the brain, often using different brain-imaging techniques). There are also numerous ways of practising 'inter-disciplinarity' (though we suggest that oftentimes what results is actually 'multidisciplinarity') via the bringing together of researchers who share broadly similar epistemological starting points. (For example, health services research often involves clinical researchers, positivistic quantitative and qualitative social scientists, health economists and statisticians; collaborative projects in the humanities and social scientists might involve historians, cultural studies scholars, and literary theorists.) But what we're talking about here is what we believe to be a more fractious kind of interdisciplinarity. This is one that brings together epistemological and ontological domains – within and across the life sciences, interpretive social sciences (those that depart from positivistic social sciences in their commitment to some kind of hermeneutic analysis; see

DOI: 10.1057/9781137407962.0003

Geertz 1973) and the humanities – that are often more profoundly split, one from the other, than the interdisciplinary configurations mentioned above. In making this claim, we are not forgetting the profound internecine battles that have coursed within and across disciplinary subfields, as well as between disciplines thought to be relatively similar to one another. (Some examples would include relations between social and biological anthropologists, or controversies between Continental and analytic philosophers.) We are also not forgetting that there has been a long tradition of natural scientists (e.g. those within biological psychiatry) working alongside (mostly) positivist social scientists. Throughout this book, though, when we refer to 'interdisciplinarity', we are focused particularly on collaborations that bring together life scientists, interpretive social scientists and humanities scholars.

Our inhabitation of that fractious space has led to our development of what we call 'experimental entanglements' – which is our name for approaching the densely patterned terrain of research on the mind and brain, as well as for the specific interventions (experimental in all senses of that word) that we carry out under its umbrella. We will not belabour the point here (it is belaboured in Fitzgerald and Callard 2015; Fitzgerald and Callard forthcoming), but 'experimental entanglements' depart from a logic of the 'inter-', which presumes that there are two kinds of preexisting things (e.g. the natural sciences and social sciences), which may or may not be integrated, and/or which may be integrated more or less well. If we are at all to make good on the current promise of interdisciplinarity, we must stop pinioning people, dead-butterfly-like, into particular slots within disciplinary taxonomies – slots, moreover, that depend on intensely misunderstood histories of (in the broadest sense) scientific inquiry itself, as well as the various intellectual practices, motivations, and affects that have only lately been distributed around the arrangements that today call themselves disciplines. Such pinioning also depends on a strikingly naive view of the actual things of the world; as if people had bits that were distinctively social, and bits that were distinctively natural – as if they were not, in fact, endlessly torqued concatenations of disposition and agency, both human and non-human, and vague, half-glimpses of which we have only recently decided to encumber with the inadequate terms 'biological', 'social', 'psychological', and so on.

If this begins to look suspiciously like metaphysics, we stress that our concern is for the practical consequences that ensue when the 'biological' and 'social' are separated out, one from the other. To this we attribute,

DOI: 10.1057/9781137407962.0003

for example, the ease with which the social sciences, humanities, and the arts come simply to contextualize or illustrate scientific research; or the bizarre separation of powers that sees something like 'bioethics' as a practice that might only comment on, and not produce, the 'biosciences'. Our desire radically to depart from such an approach drives our interest in experiment in all its guises. Experiment, as we have elaborated elsewhere (Fitzgerald and Callard 2015), has multiple genealogies. For us, experimental theatre and experimental poetry promise as much – in terms of methods, knowledges, modes of construing, and intervening in the world – as the rich legacy of experimentation in the natural sciences (Roepstorff and Frith 2012). Experiments, moreover, take place as much in the relationships that unfold between collaborators, in the interventions that they choose to make in their respective fields, in the various ways that historical archives might be reopened, as much as they do in regular scientific protocols to produce new data (see e.g. Blackman 2014). We are not naïve about the profound differences between 'experiment' as it operates in the arts and as it has been conducted in the laboratory sciences. We acknowledge that the problem-spaces opened up within the pages of a novel offer different affordances from those characterizing all manner of scientific experiments (see, in this respect, Waugh 2015). Nonetheless, we think there is more work to be done to explore how different ways of being 'experimental' can open up new avenues through which to think and work collaboratively across distinct arenas of expertise.

Rethinking Interdisciplinarity across the Social Sciences and Neurosciences was written in a particular, and decidedly partial, mode. The book is not intended as a definitive account even of our own efforts at interaction and collaboration. We know well that many will disagree with us. Still less do we wish this volume to be read as a grand statement about interdisciplinary work as such. Our desire to bring this account into the world is motivated precisely by our shared sense that the declarative mode is perhaps not well suited to the strange labours of collaboration. In the on-going, global 'workshop' of interdisciplinary thought, what follows is rather less a pronouncement from a stage – and rather more an odd, out-of-step, perhaps slightly querulous, contribution from the floor. In this regard, we see the book, too, as an experiment in scholarly production. The Pivot format is produced within a distinctive (rapid) temporal horizon, and offers a particular length (mid-way between the long journal article and the usual scholarly monograph). We, when

DOI: 10.1057/9781137407962.0003

writing this volume, were interested in exploring what those constraints would do to our modes of argument, to the register of our writing, and to the kinds of material with which we engaged. The book works with, and mixes up, different kinds of 'data' and evidence, and employs diverse styles of argument. Our hope is that the volume functions as a provocation that carries a particular tone – one slightly different from the usual 'voice' of a peer-reviewed journal article (from whichever discipline), or of a heavily footnoted research monograph. It emerged out of our own, various kinds of discomposure in relation to the interdisciplinary field of our enquiries. It might, in turn, effect discomposure in some of its readers. Rethinking interdisciplinarity, we contend, can't avoid that risk.

The view from nowhere

This book is for anyone who has been urged to do something in an inter-disciplinary way (whether that urge has come from external pressures, or seems to have come from within him or herself, somewhere) – and who has wondered, exactly, what this word 'interdisciplinary' entails. It is for anyone who has already been involved in an interdisciplinary project – who has experienced some unexpected bumps in the road, and who has been wondering how to understand those bumps, and work around them in the future. And it is for anyone, from any background, and at whatever career stage, who has some inkling that there is a perspective from another discipline that might really open one of their own projects, but who has no idea how to do something with a colleague *from* that discipline, and even less idea of what such a collaboration might actually look like. As we have already noted, we will be especially concerned here with interactions between (interpretive) social scientists and neuroscientists, but the broader lessons and claims of the book should be as applicable to a researcher interested in inter-disciplinary molecular genetics, or, indeed, a cognitive neuroscientist interested in working with a computational neuroscientist. Threaded through all the chapters, and for readers of all stripes, we have included a series of 'Notes & Queries' – a collection of short and frank answers to pragmatic questions, which will guide the reader through issues such as how one actually assembles an interdisciplinary team, gets involved in collaborative projects, manages the dynamics of interdisciplinary team interaction, and so on.

DOI: 10.1057/9781137407962.0003

One of the founding premises of this volume is that there is no 'view from nowhere' for conceptualizing, investigating, and writing about brains, minds, bodies, and their environments. Different modes of investigation carry with them different archival legacies, and conventions of thinking and writing. As any theorist of translation, or historian of science will know all too well, there is no straightforward, translucent 'language' through which any of us can present research findings, let alone arguments. As much as we want to trouble a model of disciplines in which each is confined to her own pen, let us stress that this book is written, unapologetically, by two authors who have been trained in different corners of the interpretive social sciences, and who ally themselves with social and cultural theory. Having spent significant amounts of time and resources training ourselves up in cognitive neuroscience, as well as working closely with neuroscientists, we consider ourselves to be – as social scientists go – relatively well versed in the neurosciences, and in the rhetorics through which those sciences move forward. We will do all we can to speak to, through, and with those rhetorics in what follows. Nonetheless, we do have particular networks of citations, modes of address, and means of presenting and analysing our interlocutors' arguments and empirical materials. This will provoke discomfort in some of our readers and friends steeped in other, scientific traditions for writing, and thinking and reading. But this, in many ways, is a volume about learning to be discomfited.

How to ruin your career

'Interdisciplinary Research: Why It's Seen as a Risky Route' runs the headline in *The Guardian*. The author, a doctoral student in the natural sciences, but one who crosses into several different areas, cogently sets out the reasons why being (or being seen to be) 'interdisciplinary' can mean facing 'an uncertain future' (Byrne 2014). The problem, the student points out, is the mismatch between institutional eulogies for the interdisciplinary, and the antediluvian structures of advancement and prestige both within and outside those same departments – journals, funding councils, adjudications of teaching expertise – that split resolutely along disciplinary lines. 'Trying to gain expertise and familiarity with the literature in multiple subject areas can be a discouraging and near-impossible task,' she points out: 'There's a risk of ending up being an expert in nothing' (Byrne 2014). Those most at risk from this mismatch, the author points out, are people at relatively

DOI: 10.1057/9781137407962.0003

early stages in their careers – who need to be able to demonstrate highly disciplined forms of value in order to secure a coveted permanent post.

We have come across – and indeed have ourselves voiced – many such fears in the past. And we take these concerns seriously. We would add to them our own career-related worries, which include the fear that one will be ignored or dismissed (not least if one's publications are highly dispersed across a number of disciplinary journals and books). Particularly for junior people who are actively on the job market, there seems little premium in appearing deviant from the norm. For such researchers, there is a constant, nagging anxiety: by following my interests into some strange places; by publishing in journals that have little name recognition to senior people in my field; by seeking grants with those who are positioned significantly beyond my own discipline; by slowing down my usual rate of publication by dint of spending time developing strange collaborative research with researchers who need explanations of some of the key concepts and methods in my field; and in general by positioning myself as not just orthogonal to, but very much against, what looks like 'normal science' or 'normal research' – am I (without pushing to over-dramatize the situation) effectively ruining my career? Nor are we persuaded by the bureaucratic emollient that is usually spread over such concerns. The reality is that the markers of prestige in the academy, however much managers may wish them otherwise, remain suspicious of deviance.

But the thing is: we and our dispersed network of collaborators *haven't* ruined our careers. Through this book, then, we want to dispel, or at least to dial down, two recurring thoughts that structure interdisciplinary research. One, as above, is the thought that being interdisciplinary is *inherently* risky – that, if you are not careful, you will fall between stools, have your work be ignored, and be seen as a 'jack of all trades'. This generally held position is not ridiculous, but it is, we believe, overemphasized. The reality is that, even if the old markers of achievement remain (the single-authored article in *Transactions of the Institute of British Geographers* has not yet lost its lustre for geographers, nor the first authored article in *Proceedings of the National Academy of Sciences* for neuroscientists), the reality is that more and more editors, research managers, heads of school, and other gatekeepers are explicitly looking for people – in the humanities and social sciences as well as in the sciences – who have expertise in interdisciplinary, collaborative projects. The risks of interdisciplinarity aren't what they used to be.

The second thought we want to dispel is the mirror-image of this one, which is that caution betokens staying within the bounds of disciplinary respectability. The more we wander down strange interdisciplinary tracks,

DOI: 10.1057/9781137407962.0050

the more apparent it becomes to us that being disciplined *isn't playing it safe*: the truth is that staying within the narrow epistemological confines of – for example – mid-twentieth-century sociology, while it may produce short-term gains, is not, in fact, the best way to guarantee a career in the twenty-first century (and we mean 'career' in its most capacious sense here: we are not using it with the assumption that everyone wants a permanent post at a university, but to express an idea that many would like to find some way to advance their projects, ideas, and so on). The plate tectonics of the human sciences are shifting: we here describe our own forays into one small, circumscribed niche between the social and natural sciences, but expand this horizon to epigenetics, to the emergence of the human microbiome, to all kinds of translational research in mental health, to 'big data' and the devices that append it, to the breakdown of the barrier between creative practices and research, and to a whole host of other collapsing dichotomies, and it becomes apparent that 'neuro-social science' is only one local effect of a much broader reverberation. Despite everything that follows in the book, we remain *excited* by such movement. And if cracks are emerging that we – and our collaborators – might yet fall through, still the two of us, at least, are determined to go into them facing forward. This monograph is therefore part of the archive of one moment, when those same cracks started to appear – and when it seemed to us, and to many of our collaborators, like a good idea to try to work our way into them. Our hope is that it helps to create room for similar reflections in this same space – and even that such reflections will go on to effect similar reverberations of their own.

*   *   *

This volume comprises, as we imagine is pretty clear by now, a partial account. It traces journeys that we – both singly and together – have taken, since 2008, through the bizarre world of interdisciplinary research that addresses the mind and brain. We have written it in the midst of our other research within 'Hubbub', a large interdisciplinary project (which crosses the neurosciences, mind sciences, social sciences, humanities and the arts) that we take up in greater detail in Chapter 4. As we have pieced the book together, we have increasingly imagined that the book might be read – by some at least – as a strange version of the picaresque novel. The genre of picaresque is characterized by a dishonest but agreeable *picaro* who drifts from one locale to another and immerses himself in the vagaries of different social *milieux* in his efforts to survive. Such a description could well be said to characterize our inhabitation – sometimes chosen,

DOI: 10.1057/9781137407962.0003

sometimes un-willed – of various socio-technological worlds in several countries, many cities, and alongside many individuals who have become personages, characters, and, often times, our friends. And if picaresque fiction narrates adventures in an episodic manner, leaves certain things out, and is not always clear about the epistemological robustness, let alone rectitude, of its protagonist's intentions and actions, then this volume is, we hope, a decent imitation of the genre. We include stories that incorporate the reported speech of some of the aforementioned characters, and we anatomize the emotional timbre of both their and our journeys through these spaces. No story has been invented (though each has been filtered through one or both of our memories, rather than attempts to do justice to the memories of all those involved). Identifying details have been excised or changed (unless permission has been granted from the person invoked to use that person's name). The book is built on the back of those affectively freighted stories. The experiences from which they arose told us much more about interdisciplinarity than the many books we read before and during our life spent in the interdisciplinary field.

'Every discipline tells a story', notes the historian of science Simon Schaffer: 'where it comes from, what it is and where it is going. Disciplines learn such parables as part of their induction' (Schaffer 2013, 57). The range of parables about interdisciplinarity is distinctly narrow: most of them have tended to send both of us to sleep. We hope in the episodes that follow at least to keep you awake. 'A sociologist collaborating with a human geographer', noted a commentator on interdisciplinarity recently, 'is scarcely likely to generate as much excitement as an artist working with a scientist' (Osborne 2013, 95). Well, the constraints of genre are such that we don't believe we can escape our disciplinary origins. Even the *picaro* has to come from somewhere. Let us try to convince you, nonetheless, through the labour of our collaborations – as a human geographer and sociologist – with many others from multiple disciplines – that there are forms of interdisciplinary practice that, even if only occasionally, even if sometimes fractious, even if freighted with all the worries and anxieties that we are going to set out below, even if they sometimes fall apart, are still sometimes epistemologically and interpersonally exciting.

DOI: 10.1057/9781137407962.0003

OPEN

1

Meeting People Is Easy: The Pragmatics of Interdisciplinary Collaboration

Abstract: *This chapter establishes the pragmatics of how we have actually put together specific moments of interdisciplinary collaboration. Thinking through the 'why' of interdisciplinarity (and drawing on some of our collaborators' own accounts), it situates our own work within a particular interdisciplinary constellation of institutions and endeavours. The chapter offers some practical advice for getting projects started and funded – and, drawing on some peer review material, pays particular attention to the labours of interdisciplinary publication. It concludes with a call for interdisciplinary collaborators to treat their own progress as a legitimate research object, and offers some advice for tracking that progress.*

Keywords: advice; collaboration; interdisciplinarity; neuroscience; social science

Callard, Felicity and Des Fitzgerald. *Rethinking Interdisciplinarity across the Social Sciences and Neurosciences.* Basingstoke: Palgrave Macmillan, 2015. DOI: 10.1057/9781137407962.0004.

Introduction

In developing an account of the pragmatics of collaboration, this chapter is aimed at those who might welcome some concrete suggestions for embarking on – or persisting with – interdisciplinary research. In offering such an account, we will resist normative claims on what the reader *should do*; rather, we bring to the foreground some of the resources, motivations, infrastructures, frameworks, people, and modes of working that enabled (and, undoubtedly, constrained) the paths we have ourselves taken. Many of these entities will reappear, episodically, as the book threads its conceptual arguments through different research studies, workshops, and collaborations; we want to orient the reader at the start, so that she can carry some of these details with her as she proceeds through later chapters.

First, let us note that the book emerges out of a configuration of funding and network(ing) opportunities that we believe to be somewhat particular. From 2008 to 2015 (the stretch of time during which the two of us have been engaged in interdisciplinary research across the social sciences and neurosciences), certain kinds of activities and collaborations across the terrain of the mind and brain became possible, we believe, because of particular configurations and pressures – epistemological, institutional, and disciplinary. To paint in very broad strokes: these opportunities came in the wake of (and, in some way, the disappointments of) the 'Decade of the Brain', on the one hand, and the Human Genome Project, on the other (see e.g. Meloni 2014a), around which a tacit intellectual and administrative conviction emerged that the neurosciences and the social sciences (among other sets of actors) needed to find some kind of shared language, and, through such language, to work better together. (Here, in passing, is a potential historical or sociological research project that we ourselves do not attempt: are we right in diagnosing an interesting 'moment' in interdisciplinary collaborations across the neurosciences and social sciences at this particular point? And if we are, how should one account for its emergence? There are, after all, many reasons why inter- or cross-disciplinary assemblages gain energy: David Engerman, to take one example, has stressed the importance not of research imperatives but of *pedagogy* (via both undergraduate and graduate training) in understanding the rise of interdisciplinary 'area studies' after the Second World War (Engerman 2015)). One of the core tasks of this chapter, then, is to bring that moment into visibility – to use our own experiences to

DOI: 10.1057/9781137407962.0004

begin to understand, and to diffract, a broader neuro/social/science landscape that has emerged in the last decade or so.

In this sense, rather than focusing on providing a quickly dated and extensive list of recommendations of specific places to go, and bodies to talk to, we place greater attention on how *we* progressed – with reference to some of the ideas, people, things, institutions, and funders that helped us along the way. Undoubtedly, there is now a whole range of new actors (both individual and institutional) of which we are barely even aware. Still, our hope is that the reader takes less note of *where* we have gone, *with whom* we have collaborated, or *what* exactly we have done, and pays attention instead to the *kinds of moves* – across epistemological and disciplinary boundaries, towards particular institutional and/or sub-disciplinary problematics – that have gotten us there. The chapter moves from general reflections on the motivations and structures that assist in opening up interdisciplinary collaboration, to the specific means through which we were able to build collaborations and garner expertise, to the strange world of interdisciplinary funding and peer review – and to how, finally, one might track the look and feel of interdisciplinary practice, such that that practice stops being a vaguely gestural thing 'out there', and becomes, instead, an object of scholarly attention in its own right.

Why are you here?

If you are reading this book, perhaps your appetite has been whetted – whether recently or a long while ago – for interdisciplinary collaboration in the space enjoining the social sciences, the humanities and the natural sciences. Perhaps this has come via conferences or workshops you attended, or through journal articles or books you read (e.g. Slaby and Choudhury 2011). Perhaps your research interests have taken you, more or less unbidden, to a point of crossing between the sciences, social sciences and humanities – such as legal debates over the extent to which neuroscientific findings might be used in law courts (Jones et al. 2013). In any event, it is worth paying attention to what has led you to the question of interdisciplinary collaboration: not only might this help to diagnose what you might desire from it, but it might also help to shape where you would be happy – and unhappy – for any putative collaboration to take you.

DOI: 10.1057/9781137407962.0009

One of us (DF), for example, is here, ultimately, because of an argument in a graduate seminar, many years ago, about whether or not schizophrenia could be 'seen' in the brain. So taken was he with this problem that he pursued it through a doctoral thesis on how the neurosciences actually come to know specific disorders – a process that took the form of a gradual realization that the broadly social constructionist impetus motivating his project was quite useless for helping to understand the data it produced. As DF came to realize that the neurosciences were not what he thought they were, he found himself becoming increasingly disenchanted with the dominant explanatory logics of the social sciences as regards their accounts of psychiatric disorder and mental illness (for example, Martin 2004; Ortega and Vidal 2007). Through another chance recommendation from a graduate school colleague that he check out the literature on 'material feminism' (see Alaimo and Hekman 2008), and subsequent engagement with the work of cultural theorist Elizabeth Wilson (2004) and Donna Haraway (1997), one of the leading lights in science and technology studies (STS), DF came to think very differently about just what kind of practice cognitive neuroscience might actually *be* – and, in particular, about how that practice might get traced across the social and cultural environments in which it took place. The other author of this volume (FC), in the course of co-writing an article on the use of neuroscientific literatures within the humanities and social sciences (Papoulias and Callard 2010), became perturbed that she was not doing justice to the heterogeneity of these literatures – not least when she subsequently ended up at one of the heartlands of the psychiatric and neuroscientific establishment (the Institute of Psychiatry, Psychology & Neuroscience (IoPPN), King's College London). The disjuncture between publically circulating accounts of cognitive neuroscience (which were often of the unsatisfying form: 'this bit of the brain lights up in these circumstances'), and the diverse and dynamic models, theories and vocabularies that many of FC's colleagues at the IoPPN mobilized, led her to pay much closer attention to how that space was being conjured.

For both of us, then, there was a significant drive to collaborate with neuroscientists in order to understand more about the specifics of ontologies, concepts, and also neuroscientific phenomena that felt quite alien to us. Compare this with how one of our neuroscientific collaborators, Simone Kühn (SK), explained why she engaged in an interdisciplinary study with the psychologists Russ Hurlburt and Charles Fernyhough. (We will discuss this collaboration in greater detail in Chapter 2.)

DOI: 10.1057/9781137407962.0004

SK: I was studying psychology [a while back]. I thought introspection was what psychologists should be interested in. That's why psychology is interesting: we want to know about inner experience. I found Russ [Hurlburt]'s publications and found his approach very, very interesting. I didn't know at that point that introspection was different from what Russ does [Descriptive Experience Sampling]. Now it's nice I can offer a [brain] scanner and my expertise and my neuroscientific methods.

What SK emphasizes is a long-standing interest in a particular problematic – the elicitation of inner experience – that led her to find research articles by the scientist with whom she later collaborated when she was more centrally embedded within neuroscientific than psychological research. For SK, the collaboration enabled her to bring her neuroscientific methods and expertise into contact with Russ Hurlburt's psychological methods for eliciting momentary states of consciousness; as she put it, 'I need certain skills that they [Russ and Charles] have; they need skills that I have.' Compare this with the account of another of our collaborators, medical humanities and cultural studies scholar, Angela Woods (AW):

AW: I completed my doctorate – an analysis of schizophrenia in clinical and cultural theory – in a department of English with cultural studies, an environment all but fully insulated from clinical and scientific practice. All that changed immediately following my appointment to a philosophy-based lectureship in medical humanities in a school of medicine, pharmacy and health. Within a few weeks of arriving, the co-director of the Centre for Medical Humanities somewhat spontaneously invited me to a meeting with Charles Fernyhough and his doctoral student Simon McCarthy-Jones – psychologists interested in developing interdisciplinary approaches to the phenomenon of hearing voices. Eighteen months later, Charles, as Director, and I, as Co-Director, led a team of 13 co-applicants to secure substantial Wellcome Trust funding for the Hearing the Voice project (a large, interdisciplinary investigation of the experience of hearing a voice in the absence of any external stimuli); six years on, the collaboration continues to expand and develop – producing an ongoing upheaval in my own disciplinary identity along the way.

If, for SK, collaboration emerges from carefully considered opportunities to share methods, AW's account seems to us much more alive to serendipity, chance, and contingency. Moreover, AW's collaborative trajectory is not only tied to particular projects, but is also woven through an attention to a broader sense of a changeable disciplinary identity. Perhaps

DOI: 10.105/9781137407962.0004

somewhere between these two approaches is the account of our collaborator Charles Fernyhough (CF), one of the psychologists mentioned above by both SK and AW:

> CF: Returning to academia after a long break in the early 2000s, I realized that the experiences I was most interested in – inner speech, voice-hearing, memory – reached depths that standard psychological methodologies couldn't fathom. There was wisdom in the humanities that I had to try to tap, and my first experiments involved exhilarating collaborations on memory and space, mind and consciousness, thinking and feeling. As a humanist *manqué*, I found plenty to thrill me in, say, putting literary and psychological accounts of inner experience up against each other, and over time – particularly through the Hearing the Voice project and Hubbub – I've seen how this open-minded spirit of collaboration can spur scientists to raise their game in profound ways.

In CF's account we are inclined to hear both the orientation around specific questions and methods – but also a broader sense of his own variable trajectory, and an openness to where that might ultimately lead him.

Perhaps you, too, are – or have been – intrigued by conversations that you have overheard; or you've become bored with your own set of disciplinary debates. Perhaps you can no longer ignore the gap between what you've read about the neurosciences (or, indeed, other fields) in the canonical texts, and your own empirical encounters *with* those fields. Perhaps you think there are things about the materiality of human social life that are not exhausted by the canonical works of sociology and anthropology. Perhaps you can no longer face using certain scales in your scientific studies that you increasingly believe to have little face validity, and even less construct validity. If you're a social scientist, perhaps you just think that your social scientific and humanities colleagues who circle the neurosciences are more likely to get funding than you are. Perhaps you are a neuroscientist with a cosmopolitan approach to methods and theories. Perhaps you are wondering how you might gain access to resources specifically earmarked for interdisciplinary work. What actors, phenomena, and motivations, in other words, are present in your own landscape that might open up (or that have opened up) paths towards interdisciplinary collaboration? What might you do with your own, specific epistemological and affective orientations *vis-à-vis* the potential for interdisciplinary collaboration in these domains?

DOI: 10.1057/9781137407962.0004

Getting started

In many ways, we were both lucky to be in more or less the right place at the right time for the kinds of collaborative research that we wanted to do. Specifically, we benefited from two significant European networks and platforms that preceded us: the European Neuroscience and Society Network (ENSN; funded by the European Science Foundation (European Neuroscience and Society Network n.d.)) and the European Platform for Life Sciences, Mind Sciences, and the Humanities (funded and organized by the Volkswagen Foundation (VolkswagenStiftung n.d.)). These two platforms, both established in the mid-2000s, were transformational in training and connecting new cohorts of researchers, fluent (or at least vaguely literate) in *both* the neurosciences and the social sciences. They were also both grounded in the conviction that physical co-location for a certain number of days is indispensable for sparking collaborative possibilities across the disciplines. And finally, beyond the format of the traditional workshop, both offered the opportunity for scientists and social scientists to work together to develop new experiments. (See Frazzetto 2011; Rose n.d. for illuminating accounts from two of the designers and originators of the residential ENSN Neuroschools, which include explications of the importance of engaging in 'experiment'.) A little later, we were also both accepted on, and received funding to attend, the residential Neuroscience Boot Camp, at the Center for Neuroscience and Society at the University of Pennsylvania. (The nine-day boot camp is designed to provide academics, business people and policy makers with 'a basic foundation in cognitive and affective neuroscience and to equip them to be informed consumers of neuroscience research' (Center for Neuroscience & Society, University of Pennsylvania 2015).) A confluence of temporary and contingent initiatives and institutions – none of which we participated in setting up or designing – was thus foundational in allowing us to acquire cross-disciplinary expertise, as well as meet collaborators from other disciplines.

It is worth stressing, again, that these networks represent a definite moment, in which there was a sense of flux around the relationship between the neurosciences and social sciences. The specificity of that moment is also evidenced by the emergence of a series of groups, coalitions, and interdisciplinary research arenas during roughly the same period – and to which our own forays are significantly indebted, both directly and indirectly. These include the NeuroGenderings Network

DOI: 10.105/9781137407962.0004

(Dussauge and Kaiser 2012), the people and publications assembled around 'critical neuroscience' (e.g. Choudhury, Nagel, and Slaby 2009; Choudhury and Slaby 2012; Critical Neuroscience n.d.), the field of neuropsychoanalysis (Solms and Turnbull 2011; Fotopoulou, Pfaff and Conway 2012), the Association of Neuroesthetics (Association of Neuroesthetics 2015), the BIOS centre at the London School of Economics (BIOS 2015), as well as various 'Neurohumanities' programmes in prestigious universities (Hagouel 2012). We conjecture that that moment is no longer alive in quite the same way. It is certainly not that the avenues for interdisciplinary research have suddenly narrowed, but rather that the horizon of interdisciplinary possibility, in 2015–2016, is not quite the same as it was in, say, 2008–2009. Our hunch is that the sense of possibility that we witnessed has moved to other, currently 'sexier', biosocial fields. We think here, for example, of epigenetics (Landecker and Panofsky 2013) or metabolomics (Levin 2014). It is noteworthy that neither the ENSN nor the European Platform exists any longer (although a group of junior researchers, based primarily at King's College London, is attempting to resuscitate a 'Neuroscience and Society Network' – see Mahfoud and Maclean 2015). In our particular neck of the woods, it is noticeable that there now appear to be more large, grant-funded interdisciplinary projects that address the terrain of the brain and the mind (e.g. Hearing the Voice and Hubbub), and fewer specially designed 'platforms' or programmes to train cohorts of researchers competent in at least two disciplines (though note graduate programmes, such as the Berlin School of Mind and Brain, committed to training interdisciplinary researchers). None of which is at all to say that such opportunities are now entirely foreclosed – or that nothing remains for the would-be junior collaborator save the unenviable labour of shaving the rough edges from an earlier, open, precarious moment, now sadly passed. But there is a temporality, as well as a momentum, of openness and closure around specific interdisciplinary fields. For those interested in collaboration around the brain and mind, it's worth asking the question: What kind of moment are we actually *in now* in the relationship between the neurosciences and the social sciences? How might the specific dynamics and constellations of that moment shape how interdisciplinarity is imagined and practised?

DOI: 10.1057/9781137407962.0004

Getting funded

"I can't work out if they are actually going to do an imaging experiment, or just sit around and discuss it."

We do not overstate the case when we note that interdisciplinary funding applications have taught us more than anything else about the current shape of, and pressures on, interdisciplinarity across the social sciences and the neurosciences. All of the peer reviewer responses to grant applications that have accompanied us through the last few years have provided us with insights into both the scope and limits of the interdisciplinary field in which we have been struggling to find a place. We use fragmentary quotations from some of these comments throughout the book. We are aware that some will consider their use in a book – even, as here, without any marks of identification or attribution – to be in poor taste, or at least to run counter to the tacit norms through which such reviews are written and received within a restricted economy of circulation. The problem for us is that it is precisely in the construction and delivery of these reviews, understood here as perhaps the most potent and consequential genre of academic writing, that emergent fields, ideas, and problem-spaces are variously enacted, produced, realized, bounded, constrained, policed, squashed, and so on. We simply cannot write about the emergence of a new interdisciplinary field, still less narrate our own paths through that field, without some attention to moments of peer review. More broadly, and in excess of any other genre we have encountered, they stage the complexities, tensions, and excitements of 'interdisciplinarity', precisely at the moment in which interdisciplinarity inveigles itself into the strictures and assumptions of (to use a flat-footed term) 'normal science'.

There are two current certainties in the funding of interdisciplinary research: everyone wants to do it, and no one quite knows how. In the United Kingdom, national research councils – which are largely split along sharp disciplinary lines (such that there is an Arts & Humanities Research Council (AHRC), a Medical Research Council, an Engineering and Physical Sciences Research Council, and so on) – are at pains to stress their keenness to fund work that falls between them (Research Councils UK n.d.). And even within individual research councils, there is a great desire to fund – and to be seen to fund – work that may traditionally

DOI: 10.1057/9781137407962.0004

fall outside the council's remit (see e.g. Economic and Social Research Council [ESRC] 2013; Arts & Humanities Research Council 2015). A growing number of funders are prioritizing research that crosses the sciences, social sciences and humanities. In the United Kingdom alone, researchers seeking interdisciplinary funding might look to (this is a partial list that will likely already be out-dated by the time you are reading it): the AHRC's 'Science in Culture' scheme (Arts & Humanities Research Council n.d.); the ESRC's 'Transforming Social Science' portfolio (Economic and Social Research Council 2013); the Medical Research Council's 'Skills Development Fellowships' (Medical Research Council n.d.); The Wellcome Trust's Hub award, Seed awards in both Science and the Medical Humanities, and Collaborative Awards (Wellcome Trust n.d.); and the Fellows Programme of MQ: Transforming Mental Health, a charity that funds mental health research (MQ n.d.) – to mention just a few. In Europe more broadly, scholars might look at the explicitly interdisciplinary imperatives of the European Commission's Horizon 2020 programme (European Commission n.d.), as well as opportunities provided by the Volkswagen Foundation (VolkswagenStiftung n.d.), and Brocher Foundation (Fondation Brocher n.d.), among others. In the United States, comparable opportunities are provided by the Interdisciplinary Behavioral and Social Sciences competition of the National Science Foundation (National Science Foundation 2015) or, more closely related to our interests, the Behavioral Science and Integrative Neuroscience research branch of the National Institute of Mental Health (National Institute of Mental Health 2015). With a view to finding one's way through this dispersed and varied assemblage, our pragmatic and uninspired advice is: persistence can pay off. We have had at least one interdisciplinary proposal turned down (very unambiguously) from one scheme, to be received more generously, and ultimately funded, by another. This, of course, is the story of research funding as such. But that degree of normal variation becomes, we think, much sharper in interdisciplinary contexts, when epistemological norms that might otherwise be taken for granted are often, suddenly, in question.

What, then, are some of the stumbling blocks? If the spirit of interdisciplinarity is willing in funders, the body often remains weak. Our own experience has been that interdisciplinary proposals – and here we do want to distinguish the inter- from the pretty standard multi-disciplinary – can have a tough time. Partly this is because peer review colleges and panels are often made up (not unreasonably) of people with strong

DOI: 10.1057/9781137407962.0004

disciplinary expertise. Thus a grant proposal crossing disciplines A and B is likely to be reviewed by an expert on A and an expert on B – neither of whom is necessarily likely to feel favourably towards the other, nor towards the interdisciplinary proposal as a whole. Below, in providing examples of peer reviewer comments we have received on some of our interdisciplinary grant applications, we dwell on what such comments might tell us about the possibility – or impossibility – of intervening in the field of interdisciplinary research on the mind and brain.

The quotation that begins this section comes from our first example. With some of our neuroscientific collaborators, we had proposed to run a series of brain-imaging experiments whose design would not be specified in advance, but which would emerge iteratively from a series of interdisciplinary workshops that we would run. This got short shrift: 'In my field (scientific and medical neuroimaging)', one reviewer wrote, 'it is imperative to describe the proposed experiment in detail, e.g. paradigms, number and type of subjects, analysis plan.... I did not feel sufficient information was provided to indicate the quality of outputs.' Here, we rub up against keenly guarded disciplinary norms surrounding robust research. But if this neuroscientist found our proposed experiment too loose and underspecified, another reviewer (likely someone from the social sciences) found it too concrete: our proposal demonstrated a 'naïve realism about the experiment and its ambitions for experimental convergence... [while the] ambition to establish a more general proto-col to be followed by others is epistemically naïve and unreflexively normative'. The broader problem becomes clear here: try to design an interdisciplinary experiment that puts together the empirical rigour of neuroimaging and the conceptual openness of the humanities, and there is a good chance that you will be condemned by neuroscientists for your ambiguity, and by humanities scholars and/or interpretive social scien-tists for your empiricism.

In a second example – from a peer review of a different grant applica-tion – we were informed that while our project had 'potential', we should not only do more to test our proposed approach (presumably prior to applying, again, for funds), but specifically provide 'evidence of potential to engage neuroscientists in a reciprocal relationship'. The reviewers did not see sufficient evidence of 'real collaboration with the community [we were] targeting'. Note, first, how the injunction to engage our targeted community ('neuroscientists') betrays the assumed direction of travel: it seems inconceivable, for example, that the field might be too entangled

DOI: 10.1057/9781137407962.0009

to allow the identification of a 'target community'. The interdisciplinary endeavour, here – 'real collaboration' – is set out as an attempt by one discrete 'community' to target another in a reciprocal relationship. Indeed, this comment was offered in spite of the application's self-citation of articles co-authored with members of that same 'targeted community', some of whom were even co-applicants on that very grant. Our point, here, is not to offer a mundane gripe about peer review, but to note how reviewers might conjure interdisciplinary applicants as people desirous of a relationship with some other – and thus adjudicate them on the basis on whether or not they show evidence of their ability to so 'engage'. This is a very specific *mode* of interdisciplinarity – one that already forecloses a range of possibilities for crossing boundaries. What get potentially occluded here, are modes in which collaborators are *already* deeply intertwined with people who come from other disciplines, and in which the collaboration is embedded in tightly braided methodological and affective trajectories, rather than straight-laced strategies for targeting or engagement.

Getting published

Much could be written about the challenges of publishing for an interdisciplinary audience, given the pronounced differences in the cultures of publishing, the rhetorics at play, the formalities of presentation, differing conventions around citation, and so on. As with interdisciplinary grant proposals: write an article that tries to speak across the social sciences and neurosciences, and you might well be reviewed by a social scientist and a neuroscientist, either of whom might well object to what you're doing – but for different reasons. Below we summarize material from two peer reviews that we received in response to one interdisciplinary submission.

In the first, the reviewer, who explicitly identified him- or herself as a neuroscientist, noted that while s/he had found the manuscript very interesting, it was unlike anything s/he had read 'since [his/her] undergraduate women's studies courses'. Not only was the manuscript 'incredibly difficult to parse' – which s/he explained was a result of a 'stylistic difference across fields' – but it would, in its current form, be very unlikely 'to have any sort of impact upon neuroscientists or experimentalists'. (The reviewer carefully noted that there was no assumption that the authors

DOI: 10.1057/9781137407962.0004

wanted to have any such impact.) The advice? We should 'be much more direct about what it is that [we] mean to say'. Neuroscientists and experimentalists would, in fact, warm to 'a list of facts or statements separated by periods with the occasional transition term to hold it all together'; at the moment, it was hard to '[extract] the message out of what seemed like an artistically-written piece that made use of many unconventional phrases and secondary definitions of otherwise common words'. The second reviewer came from quite a different angle – arguing that there was 'something peculiarly paradoxical in [the paper's] very concept'. We, the authors, were trying to set ourselves up as 'experimentally, experientially, and intellectually outside of the "black box"', but in actual fact, we were held captive by 'the tools of cognitive neuroscience, i.e., on a scientific apparatus'. No matter the 'depth and authenticity of the joint collaborative exercise' for which we were advocating, we were pinioned by the inescapability and irreducibility of the *scientific* laboratory. For this reviewer, the point of 'this "fourth way" of neuro-engagement' was far from clear. For the scientist, the rhetorical style in which the 'artistically-written' paper was written obviated the chance that its arguments would be received by those coming from different, scientific, traditions of research writing. For the second reviewer, whom we assume to be a social scientist or humanities scholar, it conceded far too much to the sciences. This is a fairly consistent refrain. And yet, in general the two of us, as well as many of our collaborators, have been quite successful at publishing significantly interdisciplinary papers in relatively high impact journals – a success that we attribute at least in part to such papers having a certain currency among editorial board members at some journals. We do not want to prejudge whether this enthusiasm is necessarily shared by the editorial board members of many mainstream neuroscience journals. And for the collaborating neuroscientist, being published in a high impact social science journal, which may have both a relatively long time from submission to date of publication, and a relatively low 'impact factor' compared to even mid-ranking journals in some biological and medical fields, might represent poor return for her labour. (Let's note at this point that while the 2014 impact factor of the leading journal *Nature Reviews Neuroscience* was 31.427, that of *Social Science & Medicine* (a very highly regarded social science journal) was 2.890.)

There does appear to be a growing appetite among clinically-oriented journals for interdisciplinary research that crosses the life sciences, social sciences, and humanities. (e.g. The Hearing the Voice research team, of

DOI: 10.1057/9781137407962.0009

which one of us (FC) is a member, has had success in publishing in both *Schizophrenia Bulletin* (Woods et al. 2014) and *Lancet Psychiatry* (Woods et al. 2015). See also Woods 2015.) It is also noticeable that many of our own (and our collaborators') publications have been enabled by cross-disciplinary special issue calls (e.g. the special issue of *Subjectivity* on 'Neuroscience and Subjectivity' (see Cromby, Newton, and Williams 2011; Callard and Margulies 2011); the special topic on 'Critical Neuroscience' in *Frontiers in Human Neuroscience* (see Choudhury, Slaby, and Margulies 2015; Fitzgerald et al. 2014b; Callard and Margulies 2014) – and through new, more open and flexible spaces (again, see the *Frontiers* journals). New journals supporting interdisciplinary research are also being launched by reputable publishers (e.g. see *Palgrave Communications*). As with interdisciplinary grant applications, a certain degree of mobility and persistence – perhaps beyond the usual requirements of mono- or multi-disciplinary research – plays a major role in the publication of collaborative interdisciplinary papers.

Tracking your process

It is startling how few studies of interdisciplinarity *in action* there actually are, despite the almost daily injunctions for researchers to collaborate with people from other disciplines (and in striking contrast to the numerous processual and outcome-based evaluations of working practices that otherwise dominate the arts and sciences fields). On the one hand, this is a source of frustration for those keen to know more about such practices, as well as about the ontological stakes of such endeavours (e.g. see Greco 2013). On the other hand, it presents an opportunity: it means that researchers in interdisciplinary projects have access to data on an important and under-researched topic within the landscape of contemporary knowledge-production, *viz.* interdisciplinary collaboration.

We have attempted this kind of reflection previously (see e.g. Fitzgerald et al. 2014a), working mainly through auto-ethnographic reflection. In the course of our current work in Hubbub, however, we are trying to set out specific methods for capturing collaboration *in action*. One of us (DF) is keeping a field diary, both as a form of attention to his own current project – on how urban spaces get imagined, and intervened-upon, as locations of noise and restlessness – and more generally on the work of 'collaboration' in its own right, which is also one of the guiding logics of

DOI: 10.1057/9781137407962.0004

Hubbub itself. Focusing on Hubbub's different projects, the social inter-actions that make it up, its public statements, the strategies of its manage-ment team, and so on, this project resituates Hubbub within a broader field of early twenty-first century interdisciplinarity – and the projects within it as projects suspended within Hubbub's own collaborative logic. We are also using a qualitative and quantitative questionnaire (designed by Angela Woods, and drawing on her work in 'Hearing the Voice' (see Robson, Woods, and Fernyhough 2015)), which is taking the pulse of the 50 or so collaborators in Hubbub at two different time-points. This ques-tionnaire includes a social network analysis, which will be used to track the density and dynamics of the projects' collaborations over time – and which, incidentally, draws on our neuroscientific collaborators' expertise in topological methods that they employ in functional connectivity analyses of the brain (e.g. Margulies et al. 2013). We are also designing and trialling a new method called 'In the Diary Room' – which will be an automated collective reflection and self-tracking process, loosely inspired by 'The Diary Room' of *Big Brother* fame. Collaborators who volunteer will be randomly called into a small room just off our main project space, and will therein be asked a series of recorded, randomized questions about their day, how they feel the project is going, different feelings they have around collaboration in that project space, and so on. This is one of the ways in which we are gathering data about relations of power (see Chapter 6), and about the dynamics of affect (see Chapter 7). (For further details of all of these techniques, see Callard, Fitzgerald, and Woods 2015.)

The important point is that all the different elements of building an interdisciplinary career that we have discussed – finding collaborators, getting training, meeting people, applying for grants, having interdisci-plinary papers published – are worth tracking and reflecting on in their own right. And this is not simply out of a narcissistic sense that one's own and one's collaborators' research trajectory is intrinsically fascinat-ing, but rather because these mundane actions, spaces, and efforts make up what we might call, following Bruno Latour, the 'plasma' of interdis-ciplinarity, *viz.* the 'circulations of totalizations and participations' of interdisciplinary collaboration that are still 'waiting for explication and composition' (2012, 93). To put it more prosaically: if a range of inter-disciplinary scholars begin tracking their own progress through these fields, and begin following the trajectories of the different people, things, ideas, bureaucracies, machines, and so on, that make them up – then not

DOI: 10.1057/9781137407962.0004

only might that progress, we conjecture, become more bearable; it might even help us all, collectively, to build a denser account of just what kind of interdisciplinary field it is, actually, that all those mundane actions and intra-actions are in the process of bringing into existence.

Notes & Queries: 1

Q: What are some of the basic things out there that help someone who is potentially interested in doing some collaborative work across the disciplines? What are some of the things a person could do, or look out for, in terms of actually starting out and getting things done?

Outside of the major networks and funding initiatives that we have discussed in this chapter lay a whole series of other, small, mundane activities, which were, for us specifically, in many ways just as important in establishing the relationships and interests that either got us off the ground, or kept us going. And, as we have stressed here, we were fortunate to find ourselves within a place that had already been painstakingly carved out by many others before us – who first had the inkling that the separation of the biological from the social might lie on shaky ground. We also emphasize that it is often the gradual accumulation and assemblage of minor interventions that make up the nitty-gritty of interdisciplinarity, over and above the big grant calls, major co-authored papers, and so on. Below is a very partial list of things to look out for, which is culled from our own retrospective reflections:

▶ *Residential workshops*: Small, ephemeral residential workshops, with all the intersubjective intensity they entail, have been some of the most important locations for us, not only in terms of meeting people, but also for generating and sustaining a sense of excitement around particular questions: we have benefited especially from workshops funded by the European Science Foundation, the Volkswagen Foundation, and the Brocher Foundation.

▶ *Visits and exchanges*: For generating the bonds that make interdisciplinarity possible, as well as getting a better sense of the texture of an intellectual practice, there is no substitute for actually being present in someone's working space (whether a neuroscientific laboratory or a social sciences or humanities centre)

DOI: 10.1057/9781137407962.0004

for a while – not in the (sometimes) watchful, self-satisfied ethnographic mode, but rather through more open logics of hospitality and curiosity.

▶ *Virtual spaces*: Virtual spaces are vital for undergirding collaboration. They range from actual collaborative tools (such as Slack, Google Docs, or shared Zotero libraries), to simply having a decent Twitter presence that makes you visible to potential collaborators from other fields. Twitter is also good for keeping track of a field that isn't your own.

▶ *Themed conference sessions*: A lot of major conferences explicitly invite applications to curate themed sessions. These can be excellent opportunities for bringing potential interdisciplinary collaborators together.

▶ *Taking courses*: It was only through sitting in on a course on psychopathology that one of us learnt to take the neurosciences much more seriously. If you are a social scientist or humanities scholar, auditing a course on cognitive neuroscience can be enormously enlightening; if you are a neuroscientist, an exposure to what is actually entailed by qualitative methods might be extremely useful. You could even try out one of the Massive Open Online Courses (MOOCs). If you need really to get up to speed on the neurosciences, the University of Pennsylvania's residential Neuroscience Boot Camp is worth considering.

▶ *Small grants*: Many funders (and some institutions) offer 'seed-corn' or small grants to develop networks, or to pilot ideas. These can often be less competitive to acquire than larger grants, and can be an excellent means of bringing potential collaborators from across the disciplines together.

▶ *Keeping up to date with journals and blogs*: 'Collaboration' doesn't just mean working with someone, of course. You can adopt a collaborative stance simply by keeping up to date with the journals and blogs of another field – that is, knowing the major debates, the papers people are getting excited about, the controversies, and so on.

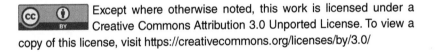

DOI: 10.1057/9781137407962.0009

2

'Which Way Does It Go between You Two?' Modes of Interdisciplinary Intervention

Abstract: *Interdisciplinarity is often imagined as a specific mode of practice, one that works by carefully separating different sets of expertise from one another (e.g. wherein a philosopher does conceptual work, and a neuroscientist simply collects data). This chapter, by contrast, radically opens up the range of legitimate modes of interdisciplinary practice. It analyses, and works through, three different, entangled, modes of interdisciplinary practice that have undergirded our own research – co-authorship, co-experimentation, and co-organization. The chapter ends with a call to retire formulations of interdisciplinarity that delineate sets of expertise and practice from the outset.*

Keywords: authorship; co-authorship; experiment; expertise; interdisciplinarity; writing

Callard, Felicity and Des Fitzgerald. *Rethinking Interdisciplinarity across the Social Sciences and Neurosciences.* Basingstoke: Palgrave Macmillan, 2015. DOI: 10.1057/9781137407962.0005.

DOI: 10.1057/9781137407962.0005

Felicity and a scientific collaborator are giving a joint presentation at a conference on social consequences that arise from the neurosciences. They have a carefully choreographed set of slides, which demand them passing the ball – as it were – a number of times, one to the other, so as to ensure that each presents different kinds of empirical and conceptual data. Each ventriloquizes some of the scientific figures who feature in their analysis of the emergence of the field of resting state fMRI; at times, one completes the slide that the other has started out presenting. It's perhaps difficult, if you didn't know either of them, to discern who is the social scientist, and who the neuroscientist. Then it's time for questions. Someone in the front raises her hand, looks from one to the other with a somewhat baffled expression, and says, "Which way does it go between you two?" She looks at Felicity. "I mean, do you study him?" She looks at Felicity's collaborator. "Or...?"

Introduction

What does a meaningful interdisciplinary intervention involving the humanities, social sciences, and neurosciences look like? Certainly we have been in spaces, and read papers, where there has been an assumption that it means someone not trained in the neurosciences participating in a project where some measure of brain activity is deployed (e.g. with philosophers parsing the concepts at stake such that phenomenological distinctions are made empirically testable; see, for example, Farrer and Frith 2002; Gallagher 2000). In this chapter, we will suggest that such configurations should not be seen as the only way in which 'interdisciplinarity' across the social sciences, neurosciences, and humanities might happen – not least because such models tend to leave unperturbed the usual epistemological divisions of labour between different disciplines.

Some of our own interdisciplinary and collaborative interventions have indeed oscillated around the fMRI scanner (see Fitzgerald et al. 2014a); others have involved in-depth work on the history of concepts (see Callard and Margulies 2014); some have taken the form of shared workshop organizing, or paper planning, or grant writing or advice seeking; still others have involved simply *conversing*. In what follows, we are going to shy away from providing any definitive answer *vis-à-vis* what a 'good' mode of interdisciplinary intervention might look like. Instead, as

DOI: 10.1057/9781137407962.0005

an attempt to broaden some assumptions about what constitutes an inter-disciplinary moment in the first place, we outline three modes through which we have intervened within the capacious field of interdisciplinary neuroscience. Some of our attempts worked well; others, quite a bit less so; at least one other ongoing effort could still go either way. In another case, a good collaboration got off the ground only after the two of us had moved out of the way. But the key is that, in each case, something took place *outside of* a model in which representatives from a number of disciplines lay their knowledge next to one another without any seri-ous entanglement in the methods, logics and principles of those other disciplines. The three modes we will consider here are: (1) co-authoring; (2) co-experimenting; (3) co-organizing. Only one features the work of a brain scanner, although even here the constellation of experimental subjects, experimenters, and technologies – alongside the interpretations of what they and we collectively produced – is rather different from what is usually attempted via an interdisciplinary intervention.

Let us stress two things in advance: (i) These modes do not constitute a full palette of options. Notably absent here, for example, is the 'ELSI' mode of intervention (i.e. in which social scientists and others gather around a scientific project in order to do the 'Ethical, Legal, and Social Implications' part of it). This is left out not because we think it unimpor-tant. We sidestep it partly because we have never inhabited this position, but also (and not unrelatedly) because we retain a strong suspicion that, in its careful parsing of duties and expertise, the ELSI mode is not only a weak form of interdisciplinarity, but is in some ways precisely the opposite of what we always taken *interdisciplinary collaboration* to consist of (see Balmer et al. 2012 for a lament; see Strathern and Rockhill 2013 for an interesting analysis). (ii) We make no claim that we have initiated these modes: in multiple ways, we have built on and learnt from others' practice. Additionally, we have a strong sense – which has been further consolidated by numerous people asking us for specific details of how we ended up doing the kind of projects that we have become involved in – that it might be useful to provide some more informal accounts of, and reflections on, our own experience of various collaborative modes, which might allow readers new to such formations to peer behind the curtain of interdisciplinary collaborative work. In short, we want the chapter, first, to augment and organize the *variety* of methods, and modes of collaboration, that any of us might undertake when conduct-ing interdisciplinary work involving the mind and brain; and, second, to

DOI: 10.105/9781137407962.003

offer some honest reflections on how, and for what purposes, we and our collaborators initiated and then persisted in carrying out interventions across those modes, despite frequent frustrations and setbacks.

Co-authoring

A collaborative bond – like any relationship, we are tempted to say – can come from anywhere, and be pursued in any variety of ways. For one of us (FC), the most important collaborative relationship, with a neuroscientist, emerged from the discovery of a range of shared intellectual affinities during a residential workshop. Immediately on leaving the workshop, the two of them began a correspondence, based around a call for articles that had just emerged, in which they considered how they might work together to make an interesting contribution. What is striking, in retrospect – and here our account is of course written from the perspective of FC – is that their shared interest in the call was an attempt to ensure ongoing *social* contact; notably, the implicit offer from one of them to the other to co-write an article was only one of various mechanisms that could have achieved such a purpose. Even more striking in the formation of this collaboration was that there was no identified research problem that the proposed co-authorship was being called upon to fill; this runs counter to many formal encomia for interdisciplinarity, in which different disciplines are often imagined as coming together to answer particular (already identified and identifiable) problems. Nor was there any legible reason why someone working in neuroanatomy and someone who was at that point based in a health services department and working on patients' and family members' conceptualizations of genetics (FC) would feel that the other was especially well placed to enrich his or her line of research inquiry. Indeed, the only real shared point of contact was some interest in a field (psychoanalysis) that was marginal to both of their primary research priorities (as well as marginal to the practices of 'science' *in toto*).

They ended up circling around the neuroscientist's field of research – the field of resting state fMRI (which measures low-frequency fluctuations to investigate spontaneous activity in the brain and hence to understand the functional architecture of the brain). In the course of the next two years, these collaborators wove tight webs of social and intellectual interest around that point of conjuncture. Without significant external grant

DOI: 10.1057/9781137407962.0005

support, they co-wrote papers, and co-presented talks, that investigated the intriguing and heterogeneous origins of resting state fMRI research (for an internalist history of this field, see Snyder and Raichle 2012). For FC, this collaboration comprised an extraordinary, new opportunity to read and think – and then write – with a neuroscientist whose generosity and willingness to open up, and explain to her, the theoretical and methodological complexities of his field allowed her to become proficient in a wholly new corner of the neurosciences. FC conjectured that this collaboration, for the neuroscientist, potentially offered the opportunity to go back to identify and (re)interpret some of the foundational papers within his field in conversation with someone 'coming from the outside'.

As the collaboration developed, these two researchers developed a paper on the current status of the 'default mode network' (DMN) (widely understood to be the set of brain regions that are engaged when people are in a 'resting state' – i.e. left to themselves in a scanner, with no explicit task instruction). In it, they suggested that the DMN would not necessarily remain at the centre of future research that attempted to understand the relationship between brain dynamics and the mechanisms of thought. In other words, they raised the possibility that the current, apparently foundational, concept would not necessarily remain at the centre of its field. Co-authoring a publication such as this opens different possibilities, and carries different risks, depending on one's disciplinary location. For a cultural geographer and historian of science (FC) to question the ontological consistency and durability of a scientific object is one thing – in many respects, it is one of the indispensable tools of her trade. However, it is often far easier to do such a thing after a scientific object *has* disintegrated and decayed – when such disintegration is clearly recognizable as one looks back at a time now past – rather than become deeply immersed within the *current* scientific and technological practices of a field. FC speculated that for a neuroscientist, who might well be, in certain respects, importantly committed to that same scientific object (not only for his own research, but perhaps also for his lab members' stability, as well as for the longevity and collegiality of collaborative relationships with other scientists), publishing such an intervention potentially carried some risks. There is, of course, a long tradition of debate and critique by scientists who are internal to their field (see Poldrack 2006; Vul et al. 2009 for two different kinds of critique within the field of fMRI). But in such cases, critique is most commonly routed through (and is legitimized around) questions of methodology;

research that gets to the heart of the historical, theoretical, and conceptual frameworks of the science are, we suggest, rarer. FC recalls that both authors expended significant energy, over the course of many drafts, adjusting the wording so that it carried enough punch for the cultural theorist and historian, and enough nuance for the neuroscientist: in particular, the many (many) annotated drafts of the article reveal, for her at least, ongoing, shared anxieties about the politics of word choice; about how, or whether, normative claims might be made; and about if and how to include sentences that pointed to the future of the field. And yet despite these risks and efforts, co-authoring brought, for FC, significant pleasures. For a cultural theorist engaged with the history of science, the opportunity to co-author and publish in a scientific journal shifted her position of annunciation from the usual disciplinary one of external commentary to one of audible authority *within* a field. She surmised that for a neuroscientist, the opportunity to participate in meta-conjecture, and to intervene in the overarching frameworks and potential ontologies at work in one's own field, might offer a somewhat unusual, and yet potentially productive, intellectual position *vis-à-vis* one of the scientific objects that is the focus of much of his research.

What collaborators cannot control, of course, is how they get read, or how they will be subsequently positioned against one another. At one stage in this process, FC followed up a shared invitation, to an interdisciplinary event, to ask whether it would be of interest to hear a linked presentation (from both FC and her neuroscientific collaborator) that included some reflection on how this cross-disciplinary partnership had developed. She received a warm reply – but one that warned her of the preponderance of 'cutting-edge neuroscience' at the event, and thus likely scepticism about a talk that would go 'too deeply into the genealogy of a field'. Some historical context was welcome, she was told – but perhaps not too much. The key was not to work too hard at 'reaching across the divide' (between the sciences and the humanities), but simply to present cutting-edge (neuroscientific) work. Her respondent lamented, additionally, that humanists were sometimes 'quite lazy' and not up to speed with the science (this writer, we note, came from the humanities).

There are many important points embedded here – not a few of which we are inclined to agree with. But what is especially fascinating is the way in which a concern about an ostentatious reaching across the divide ended up not only reinscribing an unequal dyad of science (cutting-edge, worthy of admiration, and excitement) and the humanities (that

DOI: 10.1057/9781137407962.0005

which provides social and historical context, not cutting-edge), but also found humanists to be potentially at fault in relation to a practice that neuroscientists need not imagine themselves as required to undertake. At the same time, the interdisciplinary was positioned as being at risk of weakness and lack of rigour in relation to the virility of 'cutting-edge' science. Notably, there was no articulated need for either the professional neuroscientists or the humanities people in the audience to hear any 'cutting-edge' social science or humanities scholarship. This exchange thus became a moment that revealed to FC how her own way of envisaging her intellectual relationship with her neuroscientific collaborator, as well as the relations between their respective disciplines, was quite at odds with many other, better established spaces of/for interdisciplinary exchange. Her and her collaborator's jointly authored manuscripts marked, for her, an attempt, by contrast, to disrupt the assumptions that undergirded the usual models of co-authorship and co-presentation – not least by situating the context and progress of the collaboration *itself* at the heart of any shared inquiry, and refusing to disentangle such context from the cutting-edge of the research object in question.

Co-experimenting

In 2010, one of us (DF) attended a workshop on social neuroscience, organized by the European Neuroscience and Society Network, at the University of Vienna. What attracted DF to this event was that it promised not only a *workshop about*, but also a shared *experiment in*, social neuroscience: everyone who came to the event had to precirculate a design for a real experiment, drawing on whatever account of experimental logics was available to him or her. On arrival, attendees were split into teams with a loosely equal disciplinary mix; they attended some workshops on experimental design, as well as on the actual physical logic of the scanner – and were then more-or-less left to their own devices: the task was to settle on one question between them, and design an experimental paradigm around it – with the organizers holding out the inducement that one group would be supported actually to carry out its experiment. In the group that DF was placed in, by far the most compelling proposal was provided by Melissa Littlefield, then an Assistant (now Associate) Professor of English at the University of Illinois at Urbana-Champaign. The idea was centred on the neuroscience of lie detection: Littlefield's

DOI: 10.1057/9781137407962.0009

proposal was to turn the experimental logic of fMRI lie detection away from its fascination with 'deception', and to redirect it towards the nuances of 'truth'. Given that the dynamics of truth-telling and deception are fundamentally social in similar ways – deception is, after all, always a relational disposition – the collaborators designed an experiment that would take a brain measure when participants told a 'socially-awkward' truth, in order to see how brain regions associated with that truth would map on to regions already associated with deception (see e.g. Langleben et al. 2005).

The subsequent experiment (this proposal was indeed the winning one, and the real experiment was facilitated by the Interacting Minds Centre at Aarhus University, Denmark) combined insights from the humanities, social sciences, and neurosciences: the team created a complex ecological situation (involving team-building, the generation of in-groups and out-groups, and dynamics of trust and competition) designed to induce participants, in the scanner, to tell a difficult truth about a teammate (see Fitzgerald et al. 2014a for a longer account of this experiment, from the perspective of science and technology studies; see also Littlefield et al. 2014; see especially Littlefield 2011 for a broader analysis of the science of lie detection). The hypothesis was that a neurobiological measure taken at this point would show activation, at the moment just prior to enunciation, in intensely 'social' brain regions previously associated with deception. At the heart of this experimental design was a suggestion that the fMRI scanner might have difficulty distinguishing between a 'truth' and a 'lie' – because what it means to be deceived, or to confess, is buried within a whole series of fraught social relationships, memories, feelings, sensations, and so on, whose entanglements are not well indexed by the hemodynamic response at stake in fMRI.

Simultaneously, the experiment was an attempt to open up how the adjective 'social' was being mobilized within social neuroscience – and the ways in which some deeply complex social dynamics had become sequestered within a series of physiological effects that happened to be available to brain-imaging technologies. But the form that this perspective took was not historical or social analysis (cf. a number of the essays in Pickersgill and van Keulen 2011); nor was it a critique of either the object or the method of fMRI lie detection; nor still was it a critical theorization of the psychological literature on social cognition. Instead, it was a real experiment (Fitzgerald et al. 2014b). More precisely, it was an experiment that recruited the implicit logics of fMRI *lie* detection

DOI: 10.1057/9781137407962.0005

into a scenario in which precisely the opposite dynamic was at stake, *viz.* an awkward *truth*. The experiment used the modes of visualization and interpretation, as well as the conceptual leaps that had *made deception visible* in particular neurobiological locations, in order to bring the intersubjectivity of truth to light. In this sense, a critique was made on the basis of an expertise – that is, Littlefield's literary and historical research – that is not always available to people involved in neuroimaging studies. More importantly, this expertise, and the critical intervention it afforded, was articulated exclusively through the internal logics of fMRI brain-imaging. It would not be enough to assert that deception depended on context: the point was to co-design and run an experiment that would work *with* the potent and important reductive force of the scanner, in order to bring something like 'context' into view.

But co-experiment is not without its problems. More recently, DF and FC discussed this research at an interdisciplinary workshop concerned with 'critical neuroscience' – a term signifying the desire for a form of neuroscientific investigation more attentive to its own biases, limitations, and political entanglements, and thereby contributing to a more 'critical' (and potent) analysis of social and political relations (Slaby and Choudhury 2011). The lie detection project was discussed as one instance of what we had by then come to understand as an 'experimental entanglement' – a term that we had introduced (Fitzgerald and Callard 2015) to expand the kinds of interventions that might be understood as 'critical' (see also Viney, Callard, and Woods 2015). A prominent neuroscientist, who happened to be in the room, responded to our presentation by saying (we paraphrase): 'What's critical about that? This is just normal science.' In an important sense, this is very true. Such a question draws our attention to what it might mean to intervene through experimental modalities that do not, in fact, depart from the constrained logics of 'normal science'. What does it mean for the interdisciplinarian to garb herself in experimental procedures, such that her critical impulses might have the hope of passing in intellectual institutions that privilege certain kinds of bioscientific reasoning? (For a canonical account of some of the fraught literatures and histories that we are invoking here, see Chapter 6 in Butler 1993.) And beyond such concerns, there are also of course cognitive neuroscientific experiments that do not consider themselves to be explicitly interdisciplinary, and which have mobilized the resources of 'normal science' to exert forms of critique. The famous 'dead salmon' experiment, for example, critiqued the use of poor statistical corrections

DOI: 10.1057/9781137407962.0009

that generated false positives in fMRI studies, by running a 'normal' experiment that showed brain activity in a dead Atlantic salmon (Bennett, Wolford, and Miller 2009; see Margulies 2011 for a discussion). More recently, Amir Raz and colleagues drew together cognitive neuroscientific methods and techniques from magic to demonstrate experimentally the risk of 'neurohype' (Ali, Lifshitz, and Raz 2014). There remains an open question of how – if at all – interdisciplinary experimentation (of the kind that involves the interpretive social sciences and humanities) differs from modes of practice internal to the field of cognitive neuroscience.

Co-organizing

We are at an interdisciplinary networking event, with about 40 other people from various disciplines. Stand up; introduce yourself; give a thumbnail sketch of your strengths; explain what you're looking for; sit back down. The day drags a bit. One neuroscientist, Simone Kühn (SK), in her allotted five minutes, spoke as an expert designer of experimental neuroscientific paradigms; she was at the workshop because she was potentially interested in collaborating with people from the humanities and social sciences who could help her investigate, assess, and interpret subjective experience. Cognitive neuroscience, she noted, was incredibly good at establishing objective responses to tasks designed by the experimenter, but still in its infancy vis-à-vis acquiring subjective data that captured the experimental subject's responses to the experimental paradigm (Jack and Roepstorff 2002). Her pitch piqued our interest: after all, literatures within sociology, the history of the human sciences and geography have long reflected on the 'problem' of eliciting subjective experience and of adequately conceptualizing the relationality between an experimenter, an experimental subject, and the social and technological artefacts amongst them (Despret 2004; Morawski 2007). By the end of the workshop, the three of us were part of a larger group attempting to get funding for a new interdisciplinary programme of research on 'intersubjectivity'.

With SK, we devoted significant time to planning, curating, and organizing a workshop on that question. We juxtaposed researchers from different fields in the same panel, and forced each to respond to the same provocation. (For example, the provocation 'Where is the introspective

DOI: 10.1057/9781137407962.0005

self?' was addressed by Russ Hurlburt, the psychologist who has worked for many years to develop a painstaking and extraordinary psychological method called Descriptive Experience Sampling (Hurlburt and Akhter 2006), and the philosopher and critical neuroscientist Jan Slaby. For further details, see Callard et al. 2012a.) And we borrowed from our own experience of European Neuroscience and Society Network (ENSN) events to ensure that the last day was devoted to developing an actual protocol for some kind of empirical study, rather than the event simply remaining at the level of discursive exchange. Such attempts can always fail; indeed this is what happens more often than not. But our intention was to push beyond the endless 'dialogues' that beset interdisciplinary workshops – and that frequently end up simply reinstalling the 'inter-', as well as consolidating existing positions – even at the risk of failure.

Beyond the actual curation of the event itself, some of the value of co-organization as a mode of interdisciplinary intervention was revealed in offshoots from, or tangents to, the main business of the workshop. In the course of the event, for example, SK and her neuroscientist colleague Elisa Filevich presented initial findings from an innovative protocol that they had designed and tested to explore the vexed construct of 'free will'. Working to prise open decades of black-boxed studies that have kept constructs out of the reach of the experimental subject, and that have evinced no interest in what the experimental subject interprets the study to be about, their paradigm focused instead on the subtleties of what it feels like to choose, in which the experimental subject herself adjudicated which decisions had felt more or less 'freely' selected (Filevich et al. 2013). We subsequently co-authored a short commentary on this study for the journal that published their article (Callard and Fitzgerald 2014), in which we reinscribed this nuanced experiment within some other (social scientific, historical, and psychological) literatures that had tried to think through the fraught relationship of the experimenter to her subject. SK's and Filevich's imaginative experimental intervention opened up for us new possibilities for how we might, in the future, 'torque' existing experimental paradigms that are focused on other phenomena, and that also employ complex intersubjective relations between the experimenter and her subject.

At the same event, an entirely new collaborative endeavour emerged. As we noted above, FC, DF, and SK had already ensured that Russ Hurlburt was part of the workshop; this was because SK had mentioned her interest in his work at the beginning of the exchanges between the

DOI: 10.105/9781137407962.0003

three of them. On the final day of the event, likely collaborators were more-or-less forced – via highly curated groups – into extended interactions with one another, and instructed to return with the outline of a collaborative experiment. Most of these conversations did not produce anything very concrete (and this was fine) – but a fascinating interdisciplinary collaboration, drawing together very different traditions of psychological and neuroscientific experimentation on introspection, *did* emerge from the conversation between SK, Russ Hurlburt, Charles Fernyhough (CF), and others (Kühn et al. 2014). For FC and DF, the key mode of interdisciplinary intervention, here, was to use this workshop as a vehicle to ensure that likely collaborators were pushed to work with one another – and, critically, for the two of them to get out of the way once this curatorial work was done, and they were no longer required. Interdisciplinarity, here, was located first in the curatorial labour of bringing SK's, CF's, and Russ Hurlburt's different, psychologically-rooted research traditions together (and we are absolutely committed to the view that the joining of heterogeneous psychological and neuroscientific traditions, rooted in profoundly different epistemological histories, is an intensely interdisciplinary endeavour), and generating the space for an experimental conversation to take place. But there was also a significant interdisciplinary intervention in knowing *when to get out of the way*: a more traditionally-minded mode would have insisted that, for this to be a truly interdisciplinary effort, it must include some 'perspective' from the social sciences and/or humanities. Such a view not only flattens the historical and internal multiplicity of such a capacious discipline as psychology, but also makes invisible the vital interdisciplinary labour of simply bringing things together. We are insistent, by contrast, that the generation of space, the curatorial labour of choreographing encounters, and then the willingness to know when your disciplinary perspective is not necessarily adding anything important, remain crucial, if under-appreciated, ways to do interdisciplinary collaboration.

So ... which way does it go between you two?

The answer, of course, is that in interdisciplinary collaborations it can go many ways. We have here offered three modes – but no doubt this barely scratches the surface. What we wish to stress is that the tired distinction between whether one labours 'on' or 'in' another discipline,

DOI: 10.1057/9781137407962.0005

or the desire to pin down who is more likely to be the 'object' of study within a collaboration, is surely long past the age of retirement. Let us dispense, then, with the two-pronged formulation whereby the role of the social scientist/humanities scholar is *either* to critique neuroscientific concepts 'from the outside', as it were, *or* to provide a contextualization of the empirical data that have been acquired by the neuroscientists themselves. Let us, by the same notion, do away with the mirrored image of the neuroscientist either as a sort of crude empiricist, waiting patiently for the philosopher to sort out her concepts, *or* as an external intellectual imperialist, blithely washing sociological histories away with her all-conquering brain machine.

If we understand interdisciplinary interventions, instead, as ways of marking, folding, and perturbing the existing order of the world, then interdisciplinary collaborations might take place in an untold number of ways. These could include written arguments, the performative power of heterogeneous experimental situations, and elaborations of the discursive and paradigmatic constraints within which researchers from both the sciences and the humanities/interpretive social sciences work. They might also include shared applications, the joint labour of workshop organization, shared senses of joy and rage at the decisions of grant committees – as well as the whole, unspoken panoply of ways for thinking, together, about the intersections of culture, society, environment, mind, and brain.

Notes & Queries: 2

Q: Can you give a quick list of other possible ways, however seemingly small or minor, of actually making an interdisciplinary intervention?

A: There is no easily circumscribable list of things that would count as interdisciplinary interventions. Rather, we consider it more helpful to think about an intervention as the act of *stepping in* to affect a course of action, or an issue. This can be through a variety of means – and could mean stepping in and thereby *preventing* something from happening. Many acts might, then, be worthy of consideration, for example:

▸ acting as the reader of a draft written by someone in another field;
▸ carefully setting up respondents at workshops or shared meetings;

DOI: 10.105/9781137407962.003

▶ watching an experiment that someone in another discipline is conducting (given that the act of observation can often influence what happens next in predictable and unpredictable ways);

▶ disrupting what you perceive to be the deathly curation of an interdisciplinary event that seems to be able to do no more than encourage 'dialogue between the disciplines';

▶ putting your foot down about being tagged 'the (one) neuroscientist' or 'the (one) social scientist' at an interdisciplinary event;

▶ attending more carefully to what might be described as 'interdisciplinary' differences that are working themselves out within an apparently disciplinary space.

This list could go on and on (and for some other examples, see the 'project shorts' in Fernyhough, Woods, and Patton 2015). What we want to emphasize, here, is not the specifics of those acts enumerated above, but rather our general starting point. We want to depart from thinking at the level of a 'discipline' – which then rapidly moves into interdisciplinary situations that bring one discipline 'into conversation' with another discipline – and attend to other scales and logics at which something different might take place. A mode of interdisciplinary intervention, in this view, is constituted by some perturbation in the neatly bounded landscapes of intellectual labour; it is the work of actually refusing those boundaries in the first place.

DOI: 10.1057/9781137407962.0005

3

Environmental Entanglements: Neurological Lives and Social Worlds

Abstract: *This chapter begins with the object that has perhaps most frequently underwritten collaborative work (including our own) between the social sciences and neurosciences: the effects of the environment. The chapter thus analyses a series of conceptual and methodological developments – in both biological and social domains – that have created the ground for life scientists and social scientists to begin collaborating around the simultaneously cultural and embodied effects of living in a particular environment. However, the chapter warns against some vitiated accounts of social life that can emerge from endeavours like these – and draws on recent research on the relationship between city life and mental health to begin thinking about how rich, thick and nuanced attention to the social can be traced through bioscientific methods.*

Keywords: city; environment; interdisciplinarity; mental health; milieu; social neuroscience

Callard, Felicity and Des Fitzgerald. *Rethinking Interdisciplinarity across the Social Sciences and Neurosciences.* Basingstoke: Palgrave Macmillan, 2015. DOI: 10.1057/9781137407962.0006.

Introduction

In an article discussing the neural effects of the social environment, published in 2014 in the leading psychiatric journal *Schizophrenia Bulletin*, Lydia Krabbendam and colleagues pointed to the difficulty of investigating how city upbringing and minority status affect brain structure and function. In lamenting how 'the role of the social environment has been largely neglected in the search for the neural mechanisms underlying schizophrenia', they offered the following explanation:

> For one thing, the complexity of social risks may have precluded researchers from trying to pin down the neural substrate underlying their effect. In addition, social risks have traditionally been the realm of social scientists and thus an improbable target for neuroscientists. (Krabbendam, Hooker, and Aleman 2014, 248)

Here, Krabbendam and her colleagues remind us of the legacy of a territorial division in which the neural has been handed over to the neuroscientists, and the social to the social scientists. This chapter comprises an effort to disrupt disciplines' careful tending of their own epistemological spaces, in order to figure out how those interested in understanding the tangled relations between the neural and the social – not least those whose research is devoted to understanding and intervening upon mental ill health and mental disorders – might work profitably together.

Many disciplines and epistemological domains now acknowledge that our neurobiology is intimately marked by the social, cultural, and environmental circumstances in which our lives take shape. Indeed, a range of disciplines and approaches – including, most prominently, social neuroscience (Cacioppo 2002), environmental epigenetics (see Niewöhner 2015; Pickersgill et al. 2013), and social epidemiology (Krieger 2001) – have lately emerged, or redefined their already-existing mission, in order to trace the multiplicity of ways in which, to use the *cliché du jour*, the social 'gets under the skin' (e.g. see Ferraro and Shippee 2009; Hertzman and Boyce 2010; Hyman 2009; McEwen 2012). Research foci range from interests in the role of socio-economic status in childhood neural development (Hertzman and Boyce, 2010), to the way that human social interaction becomes visible in brain function, to the role that the insults of poverty can play in the development of subsequent pathologies (Galea 2011). These approaches and areas, needless to say, have their own complex and contested genealogies, both internally and in relation

DOI: 10.105/9781137407962.0006

to one another, as well as important differences in what exactly they intend by the 'social' or the 'environment' (or the 'social environment'). We will not attempt to disaggregate those differences here. What we do wish to stress is that a still-emerging, cross-disciplinary consensus on the developmental, and indeed ontological, inseparability of biological and social life underwrites many of the most compelling ways in which social scientists (and, at times, humanities scholars, when they can claim some purchase on investigations of the social and the cultural) and neuroscientists have learnt to labour together. Indeed, it is precisely the growing awareness of the importance of the *environment* (such is the favoured term) and of *(social) experience* in understanding both psycho-pathological and so-called 'normal' development that pushes the life and mind sciences to offer hospitality – if not to social scientists themselves, then at least to some of the concepts and phenomena with which they typically ply their trade.

Let us look briefly at how some of those invitations are crafted. Clinical psychologist Emily Holmes and colleagues, in calling for a strengthened 'mental health science' that will allow '[p]atients, mental-health-care providers and researchers of all stripes' to benefit, argue that: 'great strides can and must be made by focusing on concerns that are common to fields from psychology, psychiatry and pharmacology to genetics and molecular biology, neurology, neuroscience, cognitive and social sciences, computer science, and mathematics' (Holmes, Craske, and Graybiel 2014, 288). A recent *Nature* editorial, which endorsed the importance of interdisciplinary research involving the social sciences, cautioned that '[i]f social, economic and/or cultural factors are not included in the framing of the questions' posed by natural scientists working to 'deliver wonderful solutions to some of the challenges facing individuals and societies', then 'a great deal of creativity can be wasted' (Nature 2014, 5). Social psychiatrists Stefan Priebe, Tom Burns, and Tom Craig, proposing that 'the future of academic psychiatry may be social', have argued that a 'social paradigm…would not ignore the neurobiological and psychological dimensions of mental disorders, but link them to social phenomena in the patient's life and in treatment' (Priebe, Burns, and Craig 2013, 320). Such an approach 'challenges the accepted distinction between basic and applied sciences' (whereby basic science discoveries are 'translated' into practice) by emphasizing that 'basic research on mental disorders as social phenomena would have to be conducted in the "real world"' (Priebe, Burns, and Craig 2013, 320).

DOI: 10.1057/9781137407962.0006

At the other end of the translational pipeline, Ralph Horwitz and colleagues warn that 'unless clinical, social, and environmental features that affect the outcomes of disease' are incorporated within genomics-based knowledge, the current approach may be carving a path to '"depersonalized" medicine'. On Horwitz's account, there has been the neglect of 'social and behavioral features that have been long disparaged as "soft" in measurement (because they often rely on subjective reports and physician assessment)' (Horwitz et al. 2013, 1155, 1156). The answer for Horwitz is to combat the atrophy of clinical science – by ensuring that physician investigators are not waylaid by 'quantitative models or reductionist science' so that they can focus on investigating the 'personal attributes of patients and their environments' (Horwitz et al. 2013, 1156). We are in agreement with Horwitz and colleagues. But one strand of argument that we wish to maintain in this chapter is that there has been no atrophy in the ranks of social scientists and humanities scholars: they – we – have long been working to understand the elements that go towards making up 'the complexity of human experience' that Horwitz is rightly convinced lies at the heart of understanding risks for disease as well as responses to treatment (Horwitz et al. 2013, 1156).

The social in the neurosciences

If 'the social' has never been as separate from the biological sciences as is sometimes now claimed, it remains true that there has been a qualitative shift, from the direction of the biological sciences, in perceptions of the grip that social life is thought to exert on the biology of the body. 'The recognition that most illnesses are the result of a joint contribution from both endogenous and exogenous factors', argue Satoshi Toyokawa and colleagues, implies that both psychiatric and non-psychiatric diseases are 'likely to have epigenetic etiologies that may reflect aspects of the social environment' (Toyokawa et al. 2012, 72). In a series of essays on what he terms a 'new social biology', the sociologist Maurizio Meloni roots this shift in a series of technical and conceptual developments within the biological sciences – from a renewed interested in altruism and forms of the 'prosocial' in evolutionary biology, to a realization of the force of social influence on the brain, to a consensus, in the wake of the completion of the Human Genome Project, that the genome is also 'reactive' to social and cultural influence (Meloni 2014b, 594). What such

DOI: 10.105/9781137407962.0006

developments share, for Meloni, is that, in each, 'the traditional separation between the biological and the social has become increasingly difficult to define: biology has become porous to social and even cultural signals to an unprecedented extent' (Meloni 2014b, 594).

Let us zoom in on the relationship that especially interests us here – that between the social and the neurological. The neuroscientists John Cacioppo and Gary Berntson, in their programmatic 1992 paper in *American Psychologist*, which proposed a 'multi-level analysis' of neuro-social interaction as their contribution to the then new American declaration of the 'Decade of the Brain', drew on the work of philosopher and psychologist William James to point out that 'the brain does not exist in isolation but rather is a fundamental but interacting component of a developing or ageing individual who is a mere actor in a larger theatre of life' (Cacioppo and Berntson 1992, 1020). For Cacioppo and Berntson, not only was this a realization that social processes are underwritten by neurological events, but that, in its turn, and crucially, social life folded back on the development and expression of individual neurobiology. They developed this perspective into a multiple and reciprocal determinism to insist that the promise of the Decade of the Brain would be realized only if we start to understand the ways in which 'the brain is a single, pivotal moment of an undeniably social species' (Cacioppo and Berntson 1992, 1027; see also Cacioppo et al. 2014 for specific reflections on psychiatry). There has not been a smooth passage from this generous proposal to an unproblematically reciprocal relationship between the neuroscientific and social sciences in the study of such events. It is worth noting, in this respect, that Cacioppo and colleagues, in a follow-up article in 2014 that described the potential contributions of social neuroscience to psychiatry, reported that:

> To investigate the mutual influence of the biological and social environments and the mechanisms through which these influences operate, social neuroscientists, ranging from physicists to psychologists, epidemiologists to psychiatrists, philosophers to neurobiologists, and entomologists to zoologists, have begun to work together in interdisciplinary scientific teams using animal models, patient studies, and research on healthy individuals. (Cacioppo et al. 2014, 132)

That sociologists (or anthropologists, or geographers) are not picked out in this list is striking. It suggests the need for research to account for why interdisciplinary collaborations between neuroscientists and (particular kinds of) social scientists appear to have been harder to

DOI: 10.1057/9781137407962.0006

get off the ground than collaborations with, say, entomologists. We might nonetheless claim that Cacioppo and Berntson set the stage for a contemporary research landscape that – at least in certain corners – is attending carefully to the ways in which social adversity is a causal factor in mental disorder (European Network of National Networks studying Gene-Environment Interactions in Schizophrenia (EU-GEI) et al. 2014; Hyman 2009), in which the sociopolitics of stress and trauma are situated in accounts of specific psychopathologies (Galea 2011), in which specific brain regions are situated *vis-à-vis* the role they play in human social interaction (Amodio and Frith 2006), and so on.

From the other direction, a range of positions in social theory have radically undercut the traditional scepticism that the social sciences (at least the qualitative social sciences) have displayed toward not only biological explanations – but any admixture of the biological and social *per se*. In his account of what might become of 'The Human Sciences in a Biological Age', sociologist Nikolas Rose points out that, 'No longer are social theories thought progressive by virtue of their distance from the biological. Indeed the reverse assumption is common – it seems that 'constructivism' is passé, the linguistic turn has reached a dead end and a rhetoric of materiality is almost obligatory' (Rose 2013, 4). While retaining some critical distance from these obligations, Rose nonetheless casts a future for the social sciences in which an attention to *vitality* (understood not only as a philosophical commitment, but as a deep, abiding and collaborative attention to the biological stakes of human life) returns to the centre of the sociological enterprise. Similar claims have been made across a range of contemporary social theories (e.g. Braidotti 2010; Greco 2005; Grosz 2004). In our own efforts to think with and through bodies, we have been especially moved by arguments emerging from feminist science studies, and from that literature sometimes inadequately gathered together under the rubric of a 'material feminism' – which has, at least since Donna Haraway first drew attention to the theoretical potency of the body positioned scientifically (Haraway 1985), pioneered such approaches. Put very broadly, a 'material feminism' moves beyond an insistence on the construction of gendered bodies to ask whether feminist theory might, rather, seek resources in the materiality of the body, and in the thinking of the sciences that labour to bring that materiality into understanding. It describes a move of feminist theory beyond the 'textual, linguistic and discursive', to refocus on the pains and pleasures of embodiment: 'we need a way to talk about these

DOI: 10.105/9781137407962.0006

bodies', Alaimo and Hekman point out, 'and the materiality they inhabit' (Alaimo and Hekman 2008, 3–4).

We have written elsewhere (Fitzgerald and Callard 2015) on the indebtedness of our own approach to Elizabeth Wilson's threading of neurology through feminist theory (Wilson 2004, 2011a, 2011b), and to Karen Barad's recasting of the relationship between political and physical worlds (2007, 2008, 2011). Our immersion in these literatures has led us to challenge accounts and organizational structures that separate the practices and objects of the sciences (including the clinical sciences) from the practices and objects of social scientific and humanistic inquiries – accounts and structures that we have found to be common across the landscapes of interdisciplinary research focused on the mind and brain. We are quite convinced by Barad's account that 'even when the focus is restricted to the materiality of "human" bodies':

> there are 'natural', not merely 'social', forces that matter. Indeed, there is a host of material-discursive forces – including ones that get labeled 'social', 'cultural', 'psychic', 'economic', 'natural', 'physical', 'biological', 'geopolitical', and 'geological' – that may be important to particular (entangled) processes of materialization. If we follow disciplinary habits of tracing disciplinary-defined causes through to the corresponding disciplinary-defined effects, we will miss all the crucial intra-actions among these forces that fly in the face of any specific set of disciplinary concerns. (Barad 2008, 128)

In short, if there is now an invitation to 'the social' from (some) parts of the biological sciences, then there is simultaneously an openness to think biologically from (some) parts of contemporary social theory. And if such moves are often partial and contested, they nonetheless form a gap into which the researcher interested in interdisciplinary experimentation might insert herself.

Accounting for the social

We are pitching for a grant about mind-wandering. It involves two social scientists (us) as well as a neuroscientist and a psychologist. At the heart of our bid are interdisciplinary experiments on mind-wandering, based on a workshop that will draw on accounts of distraction and daydreaming from the humanities and social sciences, as well as a reflexive ethnographic analysis of what that interdisciplinary process is actually like. Our collaborators have put together some excellent slides visualizing the state of the art in neuroscientific

DOI: 10.1057/9781137407962.0006

and psychological mind-wandering research. Des – struggling to illustrate what, exactly, an ethnographic analysis involves, and aware that he is handling this part of the pitch – talks to a slide featuring a photograph by Franz Boas of a man wearing a Kwakiutl whale-mask. We're all ready, after the presentation, to justify to the grant panel what, exactly, the hell this is doing there. But the questions from the panel, when they come, are almost exclusively *about the imaging experiments we've proposed, and are directed squarely at our natural science collaborators, concerning the intricacies of our methods, the solidity of our conceptual underpinnings, and so on. The ethnographic portion of the project (which makes up the bulk of one of the two work-packages, i.e., more or less half the programme of research), is largely unremarked upon.*

Afterwards, one of our collaborators wonders what it means when there is so much attention to what the experimenter will do, while the person whose presentation is centred on an image of a man in a whale-mask has something of an easier ride.

Our scientific collaborator diagnosed the situation, we believe, with great acuity. Here, we understand him to have been drawing our attention to the fact that while the funding panel was profoundly interested (and very well versed) in the nuances, specificities, and problematics of the novel experimental design that he proposed, there was no evidence of an equivalent focus on 'the social' or 'social relations', still less on the variable methods and attentions through which those phenomena, in their turn, might be brought to light. There was clearly room for the social to be brought *into* this space (and we do not diminish, on the part of the funding panel, the boldness and value of that move alone), and yet, beyond that generosity, there was still little scope to account for its specificities – or, indeed, to grapple critically with its own problematics, erasures, lacunae, and so on. The space was open to the social, certainly, but, for the two of us, at least, we had little sense that 'the social' *itself* might represent an important epistemological opening.

If an increasing attention to the social environment in the biological sciences can be read as an invitation *to* people in the social sciences, what 'the social' actually *is* in such spaces is often rather different from what it is within the social sciences themselves. This need not, of course, be a problem in itself: there are many models of the 'social', as well as of the 'neural', the 'cognitive', the 'affective', the 'cultural' (and so on) that course within and across a number of disciplines; such differences can themselves be revelatory to those exposed to them, and can precipitate new kinds of research questions as well as methodologies. What perturbs

DOI: 10.105/9781137407962.0006

interpretive social scientists is when neuroscientific accounts and opera-tionalizations of the social recapitulate ideas about culture and society that have long been repudiated – for epistemological, ontological, and political reasons – from many parts of the social sciences themselves.

Needless to say, there are analogous instances in which social scientists and humanities scholars employ outmoded or problematic or radically simplified concepts from the neurosciences – either to work with or to employ in severe critique of the science. We need think only of the way in which such concepts as 'mirror neurons' and 'plasticity' have been wielded outside of their home domains. Nonetheless, we well remember the interdisciplinary meeting in which the only other presentation, apart from our own, that attempted seriously to engage an account of social and cultural specificity did so by mobilizing the social-psychological bifurca-tion between 'individualist' and 'collectivist' cultures, which unproblem-atically split the Occidental from the Oriental (see Oyserman, Coon, and Kemmelmeier 2002 for a detailed critical review of this literature, from a psychological perspective). Certainly, some important notion of culture was at stake in this interdisciplinary proposal – and yet few soci-ologists, geographers, or anthropologists, and far from all psychologists and neuroscientists, would defend the notion of a 'Western' culture as a thing characterized by its members' 'individualism', whether by refusing to countenance that 'culture' is a thing (Mitchell 1995), by rejecting any isomorphism of space, place, and culture (Gupta and Ferguson 1992), or by critiquing any simple bifurcation between two kinds of people (individualist/collectivist) (Omi 2012). A number of other concepts that frequently surface in social and cultural neuroscience carry simi-lar difficulties. Andreas Heinz and colleagues, for example, lament the 'increasing use of the "race" concept in contemporary genetic, psychiat-ric, neuroscience as well as social studies' (Heinz et al. 2014, 1) – arguing that both this concept and, indeed, that of 'culture' (which they argue is often used as a proxy for 'race') carry within them the legacy of colonial attempts to categorize 'races' on the grounds of distinct physiognomies (see also the argument by the biologist William Klitz [2014]).

The point is that the roots of perspectives such as these on 'cultures' and 'races' lie not in accounts of society and culture as they have been opened up in disciplines such as sociology or cultural anthropology (at least in their more recent iterations), but rather in accounts of 'culture' that dominate the fields of cultural psychology and cultural neuro-science. In a well-cited review of cultural neuroscience, Joan Chiao,

DOI: 10.1057/9781137407962.0006

while tipping her hat to anthropologists such as Franz Boas and Margaret Mead, nonetheless figures what she calls 'culture–biology interactions' squarely within an account of 'culture' drawn from the narrower binaries that dominate cultural biology, *viz.* a literature that bifurcates 'cultures' along axes of *'individualism–collectivism, uncertainty avoidance, power distance, long-term/short-term orientation, and masculinity/femininity'* (Chiao 2009, 288, 291; italics in original). Such binaries risk rendering static and inflexible apparent 'traits' that are seen to characterize particular groups of people ('cultures', 'races', 'genders') (see the critique by Martínez Mateo et al. 2012). What gets – or can get – neurologically accounted for, as aspects of the social environment, is here already radically constrained, and constrained precisely because it has not set foot outside the bounds of a particular kind of psychological thought. 'Psychology as a hub science', Chiao concludes her review, 'stands in a natural position to merge the scientific study of culture and biology by harnessing theories and methods from every area of psychology, from evolutionary and cognitive to cultural and developmental' (Chiao 2009, 300); such a perimeter seems to cut from consideration all those other disciplinary locations in which both culture and biology have been the focus of intense conceptual and empirical investigation.

As Svenja Matusall and her colleagues remind us, the specific form of 'the social' on offer in 'social neuroscience' can be rather a dispiriting one: 'currently, in neuroscience', they point out, 'the concept of "social" is a relatively static factor in experimentation … The approach towards studying the social via communal genetic make-up or individuals' brains is rather different from studying the external conditions for a social structure' (Matusall, Kaufmann, and Christen 2011, 14–15). In other words, there is a big difference between an experiment that differentiates (social) groups purely on account of their different physiological attributes, and one that explores how those differences might be produced through social as well as physiological patternings and dynamics. One might make, here, a lament – and others have done so – about the violence that fields crossing the neuroscientific with the social/environmental can sometimes inflict upon the hard-wrought claims of culture and society (e.g. Leys 2011). Indeed, one might well claim that not only is there not an especially enticing invitation *to* social scientists, from a neuroscientific field that imagines itself 'social' or 'cultural' – but that, worse, such fields, through powerfully reductive methodological and conceptual strategies, inflict significant damage on those very concepts.

DOI: 10.1057/9781137407962.0006

If we sometimes find ourselves in sympathy with such arguments, still we are loathe to wave yet another scrawny sociological fist in the general direction of the social neurosciences. What we have tried to do, instead, through the projects that we have been involved in, is to take seriously the question of which accounts of the social are on offer in the interdisciplinary neurosciences today (cf. Young 2011, 2012) – and to think, at the same time, about the value that might be placed on broader, livelier ways of working and thinking this notion. In this sense, we are trying to work through strategies through which more compelling accounts of the environment, of society, of culture, of milieu (to use the technical term of Goldstein 1995 [1934]) might yet get pulled through laboratory-based neurobiological studies. Because, as Svenja Matusall also reminds us, we can trace rather different accounts of the 'social' even within the relatively small world of social neuroscience – which is to say, this field is *itself* contested in various ways (Matusall 2013). The tension between the rather open account of the 'social' that appears in Cacioppo and Berntson, and the thinner, more vitiated descendant of that account that we read in much subsequent psychological work is sobering. The question, then, becomes: through which methods, strategies, and concepts, through which forms of alliance, and in relation to which research questions might these thicker and more capacious accounts of social life be mobilized and operationalized? To the extent that 'the social' or 'the cultural' is a way in to at least some forms of interdisciplinarity, how do you – whatever discipline you come from – get involved in projects where invigorating ways of conjuring one or both are centrally at stake?

The urban brain

One of the – many – uncomfortable facts about collaboration is that some kind of strategic reduction (of one's own concepts and immediate intellectual ambitions) is often the price of entry. One of our core messages is that learning to become an interdisciplinarian means coming to terms with that price. We would suggest, entirely seriously, and without prejudice, that any social scientist who is committed to writing 12,000-word papers on different genealogies of 'the social', or who doesn't think she could bear the epistemic violence of using a construct like 'SES' (socioeconomic status) as a proxy for dense inter-lacings of class, social position, and education, is probably as well off not moving much beyond her

DOI: 10.1057/9781137407962.0006

sociology or anthropology department. By the same token, any neuro-scientist who is unwilling to look beyond standard social-psychological literatures for accounts of 'culture' are equally advised to stay within (or accept that she is already staying within) the secure boundaries of a well-established, and singular, paradigm.

With that allowed, the mundane fact is that there are interdisciplinary projects where better and worse accounts and operationalizations of the social and of the cultural are on offer. One place to which we have turned for inspiration is the group of interdisciplinary researchers from the neurosciences and social sciences who are putting pressure on how sex and gender are conceptualized and operationalized in neuroscientific research (for a broad review, see Schmitz and Höppner 2014b). Anelis Kaiser and colleagues, for example, in a careful review of sex/gender differences that have been detected using fMRI, have demonstrated that focusing on sex/gender as a variable leads irrevocably to the detection of *differences* rather than similarities (Kaiser et al. 2009) – and have reflected on the epistemological and political implications of emphasiz-ing such gender differences. Others have challenged core psychological constructs used within social and cultural neuroscience – see for exam-ple Daphna Joel and colleagues' study that challenged the category of 'core gender identity', which is frequently employed in neuroscientific studies (Joel et al. 2014). Or consider the work of those critical neuroscientists such as Suparna Choudhury, Lawrence Kirmayer, and Rebecca Seligman, who have mobilized the resources of anthropology and transcultural psychiatry alongside those of cognitive neuroscience to develop and operationalize less enervating accounts of the 'cultural' (Choudhury 2010; Seligman and Brown 2010; Seligman, Choudhury, and Kirmayer forthcoming; Seligman and Kirmayer 2008). Seligman and Brown, for example, have drawn on anthropological evidence to show that dissociative states are not only 'pseudo-adaptive' responses to stress, as they are frequently imagined in Euro-American psychiatric literatures, but can also be willingly inhabited, bringing to the fore 'forms of consciousness that allow individuals to enact alternative selves' (Seligman and Brown 2010, 134). This anthropologically influenced account of dissociation, moreover, can be used to parse neuroscientific data on the relationship between such dissociative states and inhibitory mechanisms, thus showing how anthropological evidence might be used to expand, torque and complicate neuropsychiatric data – without losing its specificity or force.

DOI: 10.1057/9781137407962.0006

We conclude this chapter by describing a project, whose contours we know particularly well, in which one relatively capacious account of the social is in play. The genesis of this project lay in three social scientists (Nikolas Rose, Ilina Singh, and DF) thinking through the long and tangled literature on the history of mental disorder in cities – focusing in particular on how the relations between the social and biological get recast in a range of different areas (see Fitzgerald, Rose, and Singh forthcoming, which provides a formal account of the thinking behind this project; cf. Singh 2012; Rose 2013). At the outset of this project, these three collaborators were each, in different ways, fascinated by a series of papers that had recently come out of the laboratory of the German neuroscientist and psychiatrist Andreas Meyer-Lindenberg – which purported to show, for the first time, and using brain-imaging methods, a biological mechanism through which the stress of urban life could be translated into a clinical pathology (Lederbogen et al. 2011; Meyer-Lindenberg and Tost 2012). City living has been associated with mental illness for at least a century: since the very emergence of psychiatric epidemiology (indeed, this is in some ways the founding insight of psychiatric epidemiology), we have known that mental illness associates with city life (Lewis and Booth 1994). And yet, despite a long and deep research literature, and despite the consistency of this finding, no one really knows why this is. There is no scholarly consensus around the classic debate between social causation (city living makes people mentally ill) and social drift (people who are already mentally ill tend to end up in cities for various reasons), while a long-standing literature on the 'social determinants' of urban mental illness has morphed into attention being given to the neurobiological and epigenetic mechanisms through which the tumult of city life gets into the skull.

Here, then, an interdisciplinary problem-space begins to emerge. Because not only is the relationship between urban space and mental health a well-known research area in epidemiology and social psychiatry: it also has a rich – but less storied – history in sociology too. Indeed, the question of the metropolis and mental life has classical antecedents in sociology (Simmel 2002 [1903]), while the question of 'mental disorders in urban areas' comprised one of the foundational research questions of American sociology (Faris and Dunham 1939). But what is more remarkable is this attention, and this link, to the biological and psychiatric sciences is, if not exactly forgotten, certainly not at the forefront of contemporary sociology.

DOI: 10.1057/9781137407962.0006

The 'urban brain lab' was developed at King's College London to work creatively with those heterogeneous and overlapping histories. Specifically, and precisely with a view to bring a simultaneously social and biological attention to the problem of urban mental health, the lab worked to assemble sociologists, neuroscientists, psychiatrists, epidemiologists, anthropologists, geographers, historians, and others around the question of urban mental illness – in order to develop novel conceptual and empirical projects. Distinct from much interdisciplinary research – which includes some, limited, social 'element' – the subterranean history of sociological attention to this question licensed the mobilization of sociological methods, histories, and concepts at the heart of the endeavour. Thus, at stake in this work is not the feeding in of sociological expertise *into* a neuroscientific project as such, but rather a bringing of the neurosciences into those questions – conceptual and empirical – that are preoccupying sociologists and those in proximate fields. What we would call the *sociological* social was, then, built into this project from the outset.

During 2014 and 2015, the lab ran two interdisciplinary events in London, which (a) drew together a range of psychiatric, biological, sociological, and historical attention to this question; but also (b) drove such attention, simultaneously, through the shared co-design of a novel empirical project for locating urban mental illness as a phenomenon that is lived on the streets as much as it is experienced in the body. The design of that project is, as we write, ongoing; but we hope that it may ultimately become a space for foregrounding at least one kind of sociological attention to the 'environment', and the pressure it exerts, in all its contest and complexity, *through* a nuanced and sophisticated attention to the embodiment of urban stress. It may show us, then, that even if we do sometimes encounter thin sociologies at the heart of avowedly interdisciplinary projects, there is no *necessary* relation between interdisciplinarity and vitiation. There are archives – historical and contemporary – that may yet help us to think and practise otherwise.

Notes & Queries: 3

Q: A lot of my geographical and anthropological research has been preoccupied with socio-spatial configurations of different kinds of landscapes – both urban and rural. How might this be of interest to interdisciplinary researchers addressing the mind and brain?

DOI: 10.1057/9781137407962.0006

Or:

Q: *As a neuroscientist, I feel confident about how my field models genetic interactions, but it seems to me that accounts of social risk factors and life events are often much less robustly specified. Are there opportunities to work collaboratively across the disciplines on these questions?*

A: In response to both of you, we emphasize that there are many compelling points of intersection of the neural and the social that might draw you into interdisciplinary collaborations. Here are a few of the many arenas that we think would benefit from greater interdisciplinary attention.

▸ *Working up the complex intersections between environment, trauma, and mental ill health/psychosis.* There is a growing body of evidence that links traumatic and other kinds of adverse experiences to the development of psychosis and other forms of mental illness (Varese et al. 2012). Researchers of all stripes know, however, that acquiring robust assessments of traumatic experiences is a very difficult task. There are many rich models of trauma in all its heterogeneity within the social sciences and humanities that attend to trauma's complex temporal structure, as well as the difficulties surrounding assessments of the veridicality of these experiences. How might these be threaded into clinical and epidemiological studies?

▸ *Refining modelling of the environment in animal research.* Many translational researchers have commented on the need for more ecologically valid models (particularly regarding the environment) in animal research (e.g. Nestler and Hyman 2010). Social scientists and historians of science and medicine have provided rigorous analyses of the assumptions and constraints built into models of the environment (Ankeny et al. 2014; Davies 2010; Ramsden 2011). How might these analyses be fed back into – and thereby refine – existing animal models?

▸ *Improving models of stress as they entwine the physiological, the psychological, and the social.* Neuroscientists know that there are multiple ways in which stress can affect brain function (e.g. Ganzel, Morris, and Wethington 2010). But while vulnerability factors have been extensively researched in relation to emotion, the relation between social behaviours and social brain function is far less well understood (Sandi and Haller 2015). In addition to large bodies of social scientific literature on how to conceptualize

DOI: 10.105/9781137407962.0006

and study social behaviours, there has been significant historical and sociological research on the heterogeneous concept of stress as it moves between the physiological, psychological, and social (Cantor and Ramsden 2014; Jackson 2013). How might these different bodies of research be better brought together?

▶ *Contributing to theorizations of – and operationalizations of – 'human experience' that work simultaneously with neurological and socio-cultural data* to develop new theoretical models and new experimental paradigms. One good example is the Hearing the Voice project – which focuses on the experience of hearing a voice in the absence of any speaker (often referred to as auditory hallucinations in psychiatry). Researchers have been bringing together phenomenological and other kinds of material from the humanities into neuroscientific and psychological models of voice hearing (e.g. Woods et al. 2014).

▶ *Addictions.* Anthropologists and other social scientists have argued for the importance of understanding the complexities of milieu and of trajectories of addiction (Raikhel 2015). Daniel Lende – one of the main proponents of the field of neuroanthropology (Lende and Downey 2012) – has shown how such a project becomes possible by bringing together biological measures and ethnographic data (Lende 2005).

▶ *Modelling race, culture, gender, and sexuality.* There are many ways in which the insights of the humanities and interpretive social sciences might bear on current thin (if not problematic) ways of categorizing individual and social identity in neuroscientific studies. We have already mentioned Joel and colleagues' work that pushes beyond existing psychological models of 'core gender identity' (Joel et al. 2014). Similarly, neuroscientific studies are beginning to add to and expand our accounts of how race operates and is mobilized as a social category (Kubota, Banaji, and Phelps 2012).

▶ *Linking patterns of disorder or particular diagnoses to specific histories in particular areas.* Sandro Galea's research in Detroit demonstrates how patterns of disorder or particular diagnoses can be traced to specific histories in particular areas (Galea 2011). How might historical sociologists and epidemiologists work together to develop other investigations into the entwinement of embodied stress and political histories?

DOI: 10.1057/9781137407962.0006

▶ *Poverty.* Research attempting to model the subjective insults incurred through poverty so as to understand how the effects of poverty 'get under the skin' often turn to ethological models (e.g. by exploring the effects of status hierarchies; see Sapolsky 2005). How might richer sociological, anthropological, and cultural-theoretical accounts – which attend to the complex ways in which poverty is produced and sustained – transform those models?

DOI: 10.1057/9781137407962.0006

4

States of Rest: Interdisciplinary Experiments

Abstract: *This chapter represents a hinge in the book, moving from the more pragmatic material in its first half to the more conceptual work that we take up in the second half. The chapter is centred around the interdisciplinary project from where we both write – Hubbub, a Wellcome Trust funded project that opens up 'rest' as a simultaneously biological, psychological, social, historical, and cultural object. The chapter offers two accounts of how Hubbub came about, focusing first on individuals, and their shared work, and, second, on the institutions and funders that have intersected with that work. The chapter closes by making clear some of the intellectual tensions that nonetheless run through Hubbub, as it works through different registers of intellectual practice.*

Keywords: collaboration; Hubbub; interdisciplinarity; neuroscience; rest; social science

Callard, Felicity and Des Fitzgerald. *Rethinking Interdisciplinarity across the Social Sciences and Neurosciences.* Basingstoke: Palgrave Macmillan, 2015. DOI: 10.1057/9781137407962.0007.

Introduction

We have been asked, many times, by researchers of all stripes, how we have put our 'interdisciplinary projects' together. In this chapter, we focus neither on particular elements or episodes of interdisciplinary working (see Chapters 1–2), nor on the broader problematics that are reshaping the landscape of interdisciplinary research that addresses the 'bio' and the 'social' (see Chapter 3), but instead give some sustained attention to how one large interdisciplinary project, Hubbub, directed by FC (and in which DF is one of many collaborators) came into existence. In what follows, we describe the transformation of a number of nascent, fragmentary germs of ideas into a large, unruly collaborative – and ongoing – project, which is investigating rest and its opposites in neuroscience, mental health, the arts and the everyday, and which is based in The Hub at Wellcome Collection from October 2014 until July 2016. (The project was the outcome of a specific, innovative grant call from The Wellcome Trust for interdisciplinary research projects addressing health and wellbeing to apply to inhabit the specially designed space, 'The Hub', for 22-month residencies. Hubbub was selected through a competitive application process as the first residency. For additional contextual details, see Callard, Fitzgerald, and Woods 2015.)

Hubbub offers a crucible in which we might transform our observations and prescriptions about interdisciplinarity across the social sciences and the neurosciences, which we set out in this volume, into a live, interdisciplinary project – as well as in which we might observe the differences and continuities between our plans and prescriptions, and their implementation through material spaces and topologies, particular people, and a given time period. The account that follows is one that has not been shaved clean of texture, abrasions, frayings, and fractures. (We stress it is very much an account diffracted through the interests and memories of the two of us; the co-investigators of the project, as well as the many other collaborators, would undoubtedly provide very different accounts.) Our intent is to thread some of the preoccupations of this book – *vis-à-vis* spaces and geographies, power, affect, and heterogeneous modes of intervention – through our narrative so that you might adjudicate what purchase these thematics might have when translated into an experimental entanglement over which one of us, at least, as Principal Investigator, has significant control.

DOI: 10.105/9781137407962.007

Rest

This volume has been assembled in the open-plan Hub at Wellcome Collection – which provides time and space to consider how Hubbub (as a project with its own organizational logics), is curating, limning, and analysing the various matrices and topologies (see Chapter 5) that characterize the networks of human and non-human agents that comprise it. The award of the first residency of The Hub (to Felicity as Principal Investigator and the four co-investigators [Charles Fernyhough, Claudia Hammond, Daniel Margulies, and James Wilkes]) has brought with it the opportunity to implement a different model of interdisciplinary neuro-social science from many we discuss in the course of this volume. Before we narrate the coming together of Hubbub, we want briefly to outline some of the research trajectories that Hubbub is taking, and the experimental entanglements it is in the process of bringing into being.

As a project tracking 'rest' through a range of simultaneously biological, literary, psychological, sociological, clinical, historical, and cultural iterations, Hubbub comprises a thick assemblage of interdisciplinary projects and questions. These include, to take a quick sample: (1) Focusing on the ways in which *daydreaming* – as phenomenon, construct, and trope – has meandered across a number of disciplines within its own history. Hubbub researchers are pursuing both sociological accounts of, as well as psychological and neuroscientific investigations into, mind-wandering and daydreaming, to focus, in particular, on the states to which daydreaming has been (or might be) opposed or related. Central, here, are attempts to investigate not only how varied forms of experimental practice (across different disciplines) elicit, construe, and represent daydreaming, but how such practices might cross-fertilize methods used in other domains. (2) Thinking, working with, practising, and experimenting with *exhaustion* – and, in particular, cleaving exhaustion from its usual intimacy with the subjective phenomenon of 'tiredness', and with the overworked figure of a tired individual's body and mind. Archival work, poetry, critical-creative writing, and cultural-philosophical analyses are central to our investigations into exhaustion – not least *vis-à-vis* how they might complicate psychiatric and other clinical accounts of this bodily state. (3) Thinking, beyond commensensical assumptions, about the ways in which people experience, conjure, and imagine *rest*, as an abstract phenomenon,

DOI: 10.105/9781137407962.007

but also as an index of the quality of their own daily lives. Large-scale surveying as well as public engagement are central to Hubbub's work in this domain. (4) Focusing on *cartographies* of rest, to ask both how particular spaces get imagined as noisily restless, and what kinds of technologies we can bring to bear on how those spaces are actually experienced. Researchers are using sociological and anthropological methods to investigate these questions, as well as experimenting with self-tracking devices that will draw together physiological, phenomenological, and geographical data.

One of the foremost intellectual preoccupations of Hubbub is an interdisciplinary attention to the brain and mind at rest. This attention has roots in the previous collaborative work of Daniel Margulies, Jonathan Smallwood, and FC (Callard et al. 2013; Callard and Margulies 2011, 2014; Callard, Smallwood, and Margulies 2012), which has spiraled in and out of cognitive neuroscience, cognitive psychology, and the history of science – and which is being extended, empirically and conceptually, in Hubbub. Meanwhile, preoccupations and priorities from other disciplines and disciplinary debates, as well as from other modes of inquiry, have gradually come into view. This latter category, for instance, includes a collaboration involving Charles Fernyhough (CF), Simone Kühn (SK), Russ Hurlburt and others, which we discussed in Chapter 2 (in the section on 'Co-organizing'). This research, which brings together phenomenologically rich data from Descriptive Experience Sampling, and cognitive neuroscientific data on research participants' brain states, so as to elicit, capture, and visualize 'inner experience' (Kühn et al. 2014), has brought to visibility compelling insights and empirical findings that offer new ways of understanding the brain and mind 'at rest'. Among these insights is an investigation of the limitations of common ways of investigating 'spontaneous thought' and 'inner experience' (e.g. those that rely on respondent questionnaires), as well as the need to attend more carefully to phenomenological experiences of mental and bodily 'rest' (or lack of rest) while in the scanner (Kühn et al. 2014). CF, meanwhile, directs another large interdisciplinary project (Hearing the Voice). There are not only substantive intersections between the two networks of collaborators, but Hubbub, as it took form on paper as a grant proposal, was – happily – able to draw on some of the interdisciplinary methods and structures that were already being tried out within Hearing the Voice.

DOI: 10.105/9781137407962.0007

New collaborations within Hubbub intersect with these long-developing groups and methods. One collaboration with co-investigator James Wilkes – a poet and writer with long-standing interests in the intersections of poetry and cognitive science (Wilkes and Scott forthcoming) – was started because of the lure of The Hub award, and was facilitated by interests that both CF and James Wilkes have long had in the voice. Wilkes (together with several of his collaborators from the arts [who include writer and performer Holly Pester, composer Antonia Barnett McIntosh and poet Steven Fowler]) has been opening up attention to the mind and body at rest, via considering the roles of pause, silence, noise – not least in the ways in which they loop between voice, body, and mind (Wilkes 2015) – in critical-creative literary production, as well as in performance and composition. Co-investigator Claudia Hammond, with her long-standing career as a broadcaster and writer, has been interested in exploring how the experiments on rest taking place within The Hub might draw in the perspectives and reactions of various publics beyond it. Hilary Powell, a medieval historian, is interested in exploring the structural similarities and dissimilarities between monks' attempts to keep themselves from being distracted during the labours of devotion and current psychological models of mind-wandering and inner speech. Josh Berson, an anthropologist of human–material interfaces, is working to chart the technosomatics of restful space (Berson 2015). DF, meanwhile, is working to bring his interests in the long histories of biosocial accounts of cities, mental health, and stress (see Chapter 3, 'The urban brain') into contact with other collaborators' interests in restful and restless cities (Fitzgerald, Rose, and Singh forthcoming); Lynne Friedli has been tracing the experiences of psychological coercion amongst those who are unemployed, whereby what might previously have been characterized and experienced as periods of 'idle rest', are now stuffed full with corrosive demands for self-actualization if one is not to lose one's social security benefits (Friedli and Stearn 2015). Ayesha Nathoo, a cultural historian, is analysing various twentieth-century practices of relaxation. (There are multiple, additional collaborators whose research we have not picked out here.) As the Hubbub collaborative network has expanded (see Hubbub 2015), this much larger group has poured intense energy into thinking carefully about the various ways in which rest, relaxation, bodily posture, and mental quietude have been – and continue to be – construed, represented, spatialized, and studied in medical, scientific, social, and cultural domains.

DOI: 10.1057/9781137407962.0007

The origin story: version 1

We want to draw particular attention, in this chapter, not to what this project is doing, but how it came about. Here is one origin story. Not unsurprisingly, it construes one of the authors of this book as one of the central protagonists, and centres on a tight-knit group of surrounding characters. In 2008, FC was immersed in one of the heartlands of psychiatric, psychological. and neuroscientific research. She was also experiencing a certain amount of epistemological and professional disquietude. First, there was the unease she felt at how her role as a social scientist – and specifically as a person whose interests were those of the psychiatric 'service user' – was being imagined within a large programme of research addressing translational mental health. In this role, FC was someone who, she felt, was often positioned as simply *assisting* clinical and other academic mental health researchers with smoothing the 'translational' pipeline, or with 'understanding the patient [or family] perspective' (Callard, Rose, and Wykes 2012). She was considered rather less frequently, she believes, as a researcher whose expertise in social theory and the history of psychiatry might shift some of the logics at work in the translational endeavour (Mol 2002). Second, she was curious about the complexity of the genetic and neurobiological accounts that colleagues advanced in seminars and in the collaborations that she was being drawn into (see e.g. Greenwood et al. 2011) – accounts that challenged her existing, rather static assumptions about the 'biomedical'. In the midst of this intellectual quandary, she received an email inviting applications for the first European Neuroscience and Society Network interdisciplinary 'Neuroschool', a five-year programme 'involving leading neuroscientists and social scientists from eleven European countries in collaborative research and debate'. The Neuroschool was intended to 'foster learning in an interdisciplinary symmetrical environment', taking behavioural genetics as its entry point. Current methodologies of experimentation (as well as the implications thereof within society), the 'latest scientific evidence in the field', and 'the history and sociology of psychotropic drugs' were all scheduled for discussion and debate (European Neuroscience and Society Network, cited in Costandi 2008; see also Frazzetto 2011 for a comprehensive account of the pedagogies involved within the Neuroschool).

On attending the Neuroschool, FC came to know a cognitive neuroscientist through jointly engaging in experimental practices that are used

DOI: 10.105/9781137407962.007

in behavioural genetics and in which neither was an expert. In FC's mind, there was – as we noted in Chapter 2 ('Co-authoring') – no particular emergence of a topic or problem that could form the basis of an 'interdisciplinary collaboration' between the two of them. Over time, however, they pursued a number of investigations of the history and the present of the field of research in which the neuroscientist was embedded, namely that of resting state fMRI (rsfMRI) research. (While the origins of any field are always contested, resting state fMRI is commonly understood to have emerged out of work done in the mid- to late-1990s by Bharat Biswal and colleagues on functional connectivity (Biswal et al. 1995), and Marcus Raichle, Debra Gusnard and colleagues on the default mode of the brain (Gusnard, Raichle, and Raichle 2001; Raichle et al. 2001)). FC, with long-standing interests in the potency of mind-wandering and fantasy, and the varied socio-spatial settings in which they might take place (Callard 2013), was unsure how 'rest' and 'resting' were being conceptualized and modelled within resting state fMRI. Both she and her collaborator became intrigued, indeed, by how the growth in resting state fMRI had been accompanied by a rise in neuroscientific interest in phenomena such as mind wandering and daydreaming that had previously been consigned to the margins of cognitive psychology.

This collaborative enterprise was provided with greater consistency by their committing to co-author an article in a special issue of a social theory journal. The paper, FC recalls, passed through thirty or so drafts, mostly sent to and fro in the early hours of the morning – the hours that comprised a window of time before one of them went to bed and after which the other had risen. Both of them, FC surmises, were able to carve out pockets of time to pursue their collaborative endeavour, outside of any formal support or financial structures, in part because they were at a relatively early stage of their careers. They also found a creative way to work with the exigencies and idiosyncrasies of geographical distance and their different quotidian patterns. Indeed, FC believes that their diverse phenomenological and material experiences of 'rest' (and lack of rest) ended up inflecting – obliquely – the kinds of scientific and normative questions they were interested in pursuing within their collaboration. (Such as: Are there better or worse ways 'to rest'? How do bodily and mental states of exhaustion intertwine with one another? Has the scientific literature embedded normative assumptions into models of 'the resting state' and of mind-wandering?) Dynamic material and affective contours – those that enjoin mind and body, and those that allowed

DOI: 10.1057/9781137407962.0007

precarious intersections between two researchers writing, together, across significant geographical distances – were (again, this is only FC's account) at the heart of, rather than epiphenomenal to, their interdisciplinary collaboration.

If FC and her collaborator's first published co-authored paper could be said to constitute the formal imprimatur for their collaboration, it should not be overemphasized as the thing that consolidated an interdisciplinary problematic that could function as a goad, at least for FC, for further collaborative work. (Here, we note in passing the mess of what goes on behind the scenes of a collaboration. What should count as an 'event' or 'output' to be remembered, and noted, and given weight when tracing twists or turning points in the development of an interdisciplinary collaboration?) FC and her collaborator's shared interest in psychoanalysis (a profoundly marginalized field within the cognitive neurosciences) led them to a short opinion piece by cognitive neuroscientist and psychoanalyst Peter Freed in which Freed attempted to carve a place for psychoanalysis within the still young (interdisciplinary) field of resting state fMRI by tying the 'mind at rest' to the psychoanalytic problematic of 'free association'. 'Functional neuroimaging's interest in free association', Freed argued, 'seems to be happening in a historical vacuum, at least for the majority of researchers'. In particular:

> Freud and the couch are nowhere mentioned, though the similarities to psychoanalytic practice are rather striking: the subject enters the room, lies down, and has his or her head examined by a largely silent clinician using an opaque technology as he or she thinks about 'whatever comes to mind' .... But there is a sharp difference between the two fields. In psychoanalysis, exquisite attention is paid to each twist and turn of thought. ... This and any other content-laden chain of thinking is entirely hidden in resting-state studies, where the moment-to-moment cognitions and emotions are invisible, unrecorded; all that is known is that the subject is 'at rest' or 'in default mode'. .... Without a task to model in the data analysis, all that can be said of the period of free association is that the subject was 'ruminating'. Do we learn anything from this? (Freed 2008, 102)

A moment of conceptual clarity emerged for FC: this was the point – a moment of responding in her head to a short piece of writing that would likely be read by few and likely cited by even fewer – that she remembers the stakes of her own interdisciplinary desires coming into focus. Freed's intervention, on behalf of psychoanalysis, made it clear that it was, at that historical moment, by no means wholly settled how the

DOI: 10.105/9781137407962.009

relationship between brain dynamics (the province largely of cognitive neuroscientists) and psychological processes (the province largely of those trained in the 'psy disciplines' (Rose 1996)) would be understood and consolidated in coming years. FC – through engaging extensively with her collaborator to understand more about how, at the heart of the resting state field lay the problem of relating brain dynamics to processes of thinking *per se* – realized, then, that there was a great deal at stake in terms of which psychological models, and which means of eliciting 'inner experience' would end up becoming embedded in an expanding field. It was not preordained, she realized, that neuroanatomical investigations of the brain's connectivity should be sutured together with the working objects and current experimental paradigms of cognitive psychology.

Here, then, was an opening for the interpretive social sciences, humanities, and the arts practically to intervene in – *i.e. to contribute to making* – a sub-field, rather than remain an external adjudicator of its progress and insufficiencies. FC returned to late nineteenth- and twentieth-century philosophy, psychoanalysis, and psychology, so as to think how it might be possible to open up other paradigms through which to investigate mind-wandering and similar phenomena experimentally. A fortuitous move to the city near where her collaborator was based provided favourable institutional conditions, as well as intimacy with researchers from a range of disciplinary backgrounds, to pursue those lines of investigation. Simultaneously, a new collaborator appeared on the scene, a psychologist ready to reach out as a scientific collaborator to FC's neuroscientific interlocutor. In time, all three of them started experimenting jointly, both on conceptual interventions within the resting state field, and on scientometric investigations of the emergence and organization of the various sub-fields exploring resting state research. Such a process involved FC's collaborators generously introducing her to new methods and new ways of thinking, which significantly shifted her existing understandings of the history of daydreaming, mind-wandering and related phenomena. Through such joint experimentation, the familiar landscape – one in which the social scientist or humanities scholar simply depicts and analyses the experimental work of her scientific colleagues – was decisively tilted, and a new, uneven topology of collaboration and of epistemological exchange opened up. FC's capture by, and fascination with, new modes of working and thinking together across the disciplines were, in turn, fundamental to how she approached the development of the Hubbub project.

DOI: 10.1057/9781137407962.0007

The origin story: version 2

Version 1 centred largely on persons and their interests, but was, in general, uninterested in material or institutional questions. The focus was on *ideas*, on conundrums, and on people figuring out new ways of working together to address those conundrums. (We nodded briefly towards the importance of temporal congruence for the writing of collaborative papers, and the serendipity of changes in geographical locations.) In placing centre stage a search for *intellectual* quarry, whose hue became clear only in the chasing, we have perhaps repeated a well-worn story about interdisciplinarity in which nothing much appears outside of the disciplinary and interdisciplinary *passage of ideas*. Let us try again, then, in thinking about what matters, by providing a more topologically sensitive account of some of the researchers, technologies, organizations, funders, and media that comprise the scene of Hubbub.

Many of the researchers who appear in this book (either explicitly, as characters, or unnamed, as delegates at the various workshops we have mentioned) were, at least at the start of the interdisciplinary projects described, precariously employed on fixed-term contracts, who were willing (or desperate) enough to move between cities and countries in Europe and North America. Such moves were not, we conjecture, simply to find the next intriguing disciplinary location (though we are aware of several disciplinary 'transfers' amongst our broad network of collaborators, which include: from cognitive neuroscience to anthropology; from geography to the history of science; and from Continental philosophy to cognitive neuroscience). Of greater salience, we think, was their need to offer themselves up to a wide geography in which their labour power might be bought and sold. If interdisciplinarity demands the co-location of researchers with different sets of disciplinary expertise, then the stressful nature of the academic labour market – characterized by frequent mobility and sequential fixed-term contracts – is no minor protagonist. Crossings – as the literatures on mobility and migration have for a long time made clear – involve the complex and ambivalent transfer of cultures, methods, techniques, fantasies, and habits. Affects are twisted and crushed – enfolding gratitude, ambivalence, and resentment within and between bodies. Indeed, a number of our papers that we have cited in this book were written in and through – at least for the two of us – varying states of distress: interdisciplinary co-authorship can function as an inadequate salve to various kinds of wounds, as well as a way of

DOI: 10.1057/9781137407962.0007

extending and sustaining sociality. Many of our collaborations, too, have been facilitated by collaborators' material and intellectual generosity in hosting one or both of us, or of enabling those geographical moves to happen in the first place. These larger stories of material and cultural inequalities, and of complex networks of hospitality, are perhaps far more significant, in anatomizing interdisciplinary collaborations, than the epistemological and disciplinary inequalities that we will discuss in Chapter 6. It is important to emphasize that neither material inequalities, nor host–guest relationships, line up neatly on disciplinary lines.

What of institutions and funders? The decision by the National Institute for Health Research (NIHR), which was created in the United Kingdom in 2006, to fund multi-disciplinary biomedical research centres for translational research (Snape, Trembath, and Lord 2008) is important, here. One of us (FC) was able to move from being largely external to the psychiatric and psychological enterprise (in an earlier research career as a historical geographer of psychiatry) to sitting at the heart of it, via the imperative not only to bring sociological perspectives to neuroscientific and genetic/genomic research, but to ensure that 'patient/service user' perspectives were heard. We also emphasize the emergence of research centres challenging the decades-long standoff between large parts of the sociological and the biological. The BIOS centre at the London School of Economics (established and directed by Nikolas Rose, which has now become the Department of Social Science, Health & Medicine at King's College London), and the Interacting Minds Centre at Aarhus University (directed by Andreas Roepstorff) have been foundational to the work that we and many of our collaborators have carried out.

A crowded and jostling international university environment, in which there are increasingly intense demands to acquire external grant funding, has also helped foment interest in establishing cross- and inter-disciplinary projects that sit outside of particular departments and disci-plines. This demand has dovetailed with the decision by major funders (e.g. The Wellcome Trust and the Volkswagen Foundation) to develop funding streams that would support research programmes bringing humanities scholars and interpretive social scientists into much closer proximity with life scientists. We also need to mention, at least for our own particular trajectories, the invigoration of the field and purpose of *medical humanities* within the United Kingdom, which is also, in part, a story about the reconfiguration of the favoured place of medical history

DOI: 10.1057/9781137407962.0007

and of medical sociology in relation to biomedicine. For the emergence of Hubbub, the Centre for Medical Humanities at Durham University – where FC took up a permanent position in 2012 – is important as a node in an increasingly international network of interdisciplinary centres advancing collaborative work across the life sciences, health sciences, humanities, and social sciences (e.g. Atkinson et al. 2015; Viney, Callard, and Woods 2015).

Finally, it is no coincidence that the accounts of emerging interdisciplinarity that we have given in this chapter, and throughout this volume, move in lockstep with a rapidly changing and increasingly dense technological ecology for collaborative writing and thinking. Such an ecology is characterized by divergent temporalities and purposes to which each part of it is put to use. The changing shape of this ecology has been central to helping open out possibilities for collaboration – across geographical and disciplinary terrains – whose trajectories we have described in this chapter. FC remembers the first time she completed a co-authored article with a scientific collaborator, in which Dropbox (a file hosting service, introduced to her by her collaborator, that provides cloud storage and file synchronization), to her, seemed almost like a third author; for her collaborator, on the other hand, she inferred that this was a technology that was already so assimilated that it was on the point of being old-fashioned. While scholars such as Ben Kafka have analysed the historical role and nature of paper as central to the operations of bureaucracy (Kafka 2012), it is not clear whether there is, yet, any adequate account of how intimately current practices of writing, talking, storing, tracing, joking, and fighting through and across platforms such as Google Hangouts and Google Docs, Skype, Slack, Dropbox, Twitter, Zotero, and so on are bound up with the changing shapes of collaboration, non-collaboration and interdisciplinarity. It has been striking, in the trajectories that built towards Hubbub (as well as those ongoing dynamics within it), to note how there is no straightforward way in which one can map ease and interest in the use of particular media on to particular disciplinary allegiances. Here, then, unexpected media topologies – in which collaborators from very different disciplines might come together around common commitments to particular ways of sharing, communicating, or keeping to oneself – are produced that run counter to usual stories of epistemological differences that require a 'reaching across' disciplinary boundaries. How both we and our collaborators have agreed (keenly or reluctantly), or not, to communicate via particular kinds of

DOI: 10.1057/9781137407962.0007

media has told us a great deal, not only about the heterogeneity of intra- as well as interdisciplinary commitments and backgrounds, but about different visions of what collaboration, loss of control, exchange, shared labour, incorporation of ideas, and writing, itself, *might mean.*

'We've now split ...'

In presenting, here, particular narratives of how things emerge, we might have given the (false) impression that the hard work of establishing, and persisting with, interdisciplinary collaborations was largely in the (pre-Hubbub) past. Let us emphasize, then, in closing, the ongoing challenges that characterize any space in which collaborators with very different sets of expertise, as well as different understandings and practices of interdisciplinarity, work together. There is, we both believe, no singular direction of travel within Hubbub. Our collaborators do not have a shared vision of what the purpose or telos of interdisciplinarity might be, nor what the appropriate working methods are for engaging in such interdisciplinary collaboration. They – and we – are undoubtedly working with a variety of needs, logics, ontologies, and practices (Barry, Born, and Weszkalnys 2008). Consider this short note, taken by one of the present authors (DF) during an early project meeting (all errors of typography and syntax are from the original):

▸ *Kind of feels like the psychologists are having a conversation among themselves.... - what happened to the larger questions we started with? This is how it tend to go; we start off with something high-level, then the psychologists start talking through what they imagine to be the pragmatics ... and suddenly we're having a conversation about the parameters of having a psychological study.*

▸ *The issue i have is that in rooms that are dominated by psychology/ psychologists (> 50% in this room) i always feel obloged to represnet and then get fiured as representing – all the things that are not psychology. And that's an impossible position, so you aways end up syang very broad & silly things.*

▸ *We've now split [...] [Person X] has said that what holds [out half of the split] together is the willingness to defer ontological commitments, which i thnk he's basically right about – but this seems to have caused a little bit of confusion controversy.*

DOI: 10.1057/9781137407962.0007

▸ *[…]*

▸ *afte lunch we;ve split – the psychologsts have all [gone] to work [on their own] – te rest of us have have stayed in the room to […] The thing is totally split at this point. [Person Y] asks (rightly) what does it mean for the project that we've all split off like this??*

▸ *[Later, Person Z] interestingly insisting that if we force a top-dwon interdisicplinarity, it'll be a total balls (and why we've been having this endless discussion […] going around in circles); the best thing is to let people just do what they're good at, and then (a) trust ID [interdisciplinary] stuff to bubble up from the talented poeple we have; (b) have some curation at the top.*

What to make of this? For a start, let's notice how epistemological and ontological difference plays out spatially (some collaborators physically *leave the* room), affectively (note the documenter's own irritation, as well as the implication that those moments of controversy have become fraught across the whole group), and through an unequal dynamics of epistemological power (i.e. psychology's perceived chauvinism, which, on the documenter's account, allows a rapid pull away from the 'high-level' and a turn to the 'parameters of […] a psychological study'). What rings out from the note is the author's jaundiced account of what is at stake for psychologists – as well as his juvenile sense of frustration at being part of a conversation that felt as though it were dominated by the normative commitments of that discipline. But if the details are fuzzy (in fact, not all scientists left the room), the feelings expressed here are real enough. The point is not about 'psychology' or 'psychologists' (a category, in any event, poorly described in this note) but about some in-the-moment sensations through which logics of collaboration, even in as tight an assemblage as this one, are both produced and experienced. Needless to say, the collaborators positioned as 'psychologists' (they were not even all psychologists) have their own accounts of this episode. As one put it to us, on reading the above extract:

> *It was a very productive and interesting discussion, although I remember being powerfully reminded of some of the disciplinary differences. I like to think that we psychologists are aware of the endless possibilities for defining and critiquing terms, but it's also true that our instinct is to get on and do stuff, even if the conceptual framework is not perfect. I remember thinking, My God, how does anything ever get done, if we're going to argue at every step about whether everything we want to say is equally applicable to all strata of society? How do these (lovely, smart) people ever finish anything?!*

DOI: 10.1057/9781137407962.0007

Another psychologist who was present on the day remembers it like this:

> *My recollection of the day is that after hours and hours of nothing getting decided, and this being our only chance all together to get the planning done that the whole group decided the only way to do it was to split into two groups, but that's just my memory of it ... Of course I do see that the problem for interdisciplinarity here was that all the psychologists chose the practical planning group and everyone else chose the discussion group. So we all conformed to the various stereotypes. I do have to wonder whether the [project in question] would be at the advanced stage that it's at today, if the group had stayed as one?*

Here then, even as the three accounts diverge markedly in what happened, there is, at least to our eyes, a way in which the discipline of psychology, here, is positioned – or imagines itself to be – as more pragmatic than the other disciplines. We are reminded that, even in Hubbub, which is an endeavour in many ways defined by its successes, disagreement abounds. Feelings can run high. Very different ideas of the stakes of the project, as well as the modes of investigation appropriate to it, run headlong into one another. If the split in the above meeting was temporary, and indeed productive, we believe, for the research of Hubbub as a whole, we remind ourselves of the thin sutures that continue to hold interdisciplinary collaborative projects together. We remain deeply alive to our own capacity, at any moment, to come undone.

Notes and Queries: 4

Q: What is the most important element of an interdisciplinary project? The idea? The people? The funder? The level of institutional support? What should I be really looking for – an excellent proposal or a brilliant collaborator?

This is an area where our experience tends to run against the usual advice. Typically what people will say is that the problem should come first. And so, good interdisciplinarity happens when, for example, a philosopher has a conception of free will that can be empirically tested, and he (in analytic philosophy, it almost certainly *is* a he) runs into a neuroscientist who has methods that can perform that empirical test – and who, in turn, has some ideas about free will that could do with some conceptual refinement. This

DOI: 10.105/9781137407962.009

is fine, of course – but like so much else in the interdisciplinary field, it is predicated on a potentially unrealistic idea of how intellectual work actually happens. FC and her neuroscientific collaborator started working on rest, for example, because they liked one another, and shared some basic intuitions. 'Rest' was also a point that FC loosely had in common with James Wilkes, the poet she met at a funding open day, and they liked each other too – so that started to become the topic of the project. Moreover, FC was only in that room because she had some support from Durham University to put something together for The Wellcome Trust Hub award – which is to say, the support, like the desire for collaboration, came before the question. DF assembled the urban brain project (see Chapter 3) with Nikolas Rose and Ilina Singh because the three of them were thinking through their shared intuitions on sociology and biology; again, the decision to collaborate on these intuitions came before the identification of the actual research question. The point is that there is no right way to develop an interdisciplinary collaboration, and no correct order that the different elements must come in – interdisciplinary projects, like all intellectual work, are always loose assemblages with strange temporalities. If you have a really good idea, and you need someone from another discipline to help you with it – that's great. But don't be anxious if you just want to collaborate because you like someone, or you might get some support from your university if you do. The problem will emerge: there's no particular reason it has to emerge first.

DOI: 10.1057/9781137407962.0009

OPEN

5

Choreographing the Interdisciplinary

Abstract: *Interdisciplinary works tends to have an inbuilt spatial logic, based, for example, on the model of the 'layer cake' – in which each layer encompasses a specific, tightly-bounded domain. This chapter is about distributions of space and time in interdisciplinary projects, and a critique of the dominant spatial logics and metaphors that often prop up interdisciplinary endeavours. Against such imaginaries, the chapter sets out four alternatives for rethinking the space of interdisciplinarity: matrices, topologies, incorporations, laboratories. The chapter positions these alternatives as ways of imagining interdisciplinary space, beyond the logic of fiefdom that now predominates.*

Keywords: expertise; interdisciplinarity; laboratory; matrix; space; topology

Callard, Felicity and Des Fitzgerald. *Rethinking Interdisciplinarity across the Social Sciences and Neurosciences.* Basingstoke: Palgrave Macmillan, 2015. DOI: 10.1057/9781137407962.0008.

Introduction

The distribution and use of space and time is a surprisingly potent – and fraught – topic in interdisciplinary projects. Funders, institutions, and researchers are increasingly paying attention to how physical buildings and centres might facilitate, or inhibit, interdisciplinary exchange (Dzeng 2013). One of us (DF), for example, spent almost a year at the expressly interdisciplinary Interacting Minds Centre at Aarhus University (Interacting Minds Centre 2014), where doorless, all-glass offices fostered a sense of free movement and exchange. The Hub at Wellcome Collection, in which we have written this book, was explicitly designed to facilitate collaborative, interdisciplinary interaction. Similarly, people collaborating at a distance from one another will often place a premium on having tools and funds for getting themselves into a shared space, whether physically or virtually. These are important issues, of course. And yet, over the years that we have been moving through diverse interdisciplinary landscapes, we have come to realize that the spatial logic of interdisciplinarity isn't only about the physical arrangement of offices and corridors: it's also about the careful (though often unspoken) arrangement of people, objects, ideas, technologies, and media in relation to one another. It's about the choreography – the 'deftly balanced coming together of things that are generally considered parts of different ontological orders' (Thompson 2005, 8) – through which those things are induced to relate to one another, as well as the habits and modes of comportment that, sometimes, prevent those people and things from getting *too* close.

In this chapter, we will be concerned with space in both senses (as physical entity and as choreography) – but we will pay closer attention to the second. Because it is precisely this tacit choreography, this highly elaborated dance of movement and fixture, we claim, that governs the distribution and use of time and space in interdisciplinary projects. Over the years that we have spent in interdisciplinary spaces that address the mind and the brain, we have become convinced, first, that the logic of the prefix 'inter-' tends to lie at the heart of those arrangements and choreographies, and second, that that prefix acts as a serious hindrance to the kind of research that might be done across the neurosciences, social sciences, and humanities. Indeed, this deceptively harmless prefix tends to govern the suturing of discipline to discipline (often via a particular way of envisaging how experiment is best put into practice), and has

DOI: 10.105/9781137407962.0008

significantly constrained how interdisciplinary research in this area is both imagined and conducted. 'Far from being opposed to disciplinarity', Thomas Osborne points out, '*inter*disciplinarity assumes a certain consciousness of disciplinarity as a condition for its accomplishment' (Osborne 2013, 82; our emphasis). The problem for us with the prefix inter- is that it denotes both spatial and temporal 'betweens': it hence locates the point of interest *between* intervals of time, and *between* parts of things. The concept of interdisciplinarity, as it is currently practised, thus carries within it a very particular model of spatial and temporal relations – as if there were a chessboard of disciplines, weaving in and out of one another, but never occupying the same, uneven ground.

We want to break the spatial and temporal structure assumed by the inter- of interdisciplinarity. In its place, and drawing on our own experiences, we open other ways of imagining and unfolding the – in fact – much more tangled and patterned world of complex relations, and non-relations, between human and non-human entities, as well as between the various domains of knowledge that attempt to address them. For it is that tangled world – with its heterogeneous rhythms and mysterious arrangements – that is what those calling for interdisciplinary research involving the neurosciences and social sciences are attempting to understand and to intervene upon, even as they sometimes tend their own epistemologically bounded spaces. We are certainly not arguing that interdisciplinarity is found in just one form (for various examples of the heterogeneity of forms, see Schaffer 2013). As Barry and Born have noted, the question, rather, is: 'How might one understand interdisciplinarity less as a unity and more as a field of differences, a multiplicity?' (Barry and Born 2013, 5). Still, we argue that to understand the complexity of brain–mind–body–environment relations, we need to jettison the spatial logics of the inter- if we are at all to make good on the promise that interdisciplinarity holds. In so doing, we work neither with a fantasy of pure, prior disciplines that the logic of the inter- attempts to make concrete (see also Osborne 2013), nor with an integrative vision in which different disciplines are tugged ever-closer to one another (see also Fitzgerald and Callard forthcoming). We ask our readers to join us on in departing from the temporal frameworks and spatial strictures to which so many of today's practices of interdisciplinarity remain sadly tethered.

In this chapter, we are particularly preoccupied with the scales, relationalities, patterns, rhythms and voids that might be useful for understanding practices of interdisciplinarity, once we have abandoned spatial

DOI: 10.105/9781137407962.0008

logics that privilege either what happens 'between' disciplines, or that are premised on working towards their future integration. We reflect on the spaces, times, and rhythms – material and conceptual – that we have found most generative, in terms of fomenting epistemological excitement and novel ways of practising collaboration. Here, as everywhere in this volume, one of our primary concerns is with developing new forms of experimental practice that also comprise, simultaneously, new forms for thinking around and with problems. Collaboration, is, for us, 'a distinctive and changeable set of practices, an object of enquiry, a field of dispositions, a relation of power, an intervention in a space, a set of affective and embodied comportments' (Callard, Fitzgerald, and Woods 2015, 4): how one envisages and organizes collaboration, then, is far from inconsequential in shaping how both experiment, and thinking with and through others' concerns and models, might take place. But acknowledging and bringing to the foreground richer and less predictable accounts of the spaces and times in which collaboration across disciplines might take place is no easy task. Before rooting some of those accounts out, we first self-consciously divest ourselves of what we believe to be some of the more unhelpful assumptions about the 'proper' space and time of and for interdisciplinarity that we have – repeatedly – witnessed and experienced.

Have you got a neuroscientist yet?

Consider the vignette with which we started this book (see the Introduction), in which our group had not (yet) acquired the indispensable neuroscientist. What does this vignette reveal? In retrospect, we realized that it exemplified the way in which a particular vision of interdisciplinarity involving the mind sciences, life sciences, social sciences, and humanities was being assumed – by funders, by institutions, and by many of those (including, at times, the two of us) who are gathering in this field. It carries strong prescriptions about what interdisciplinary research in this field is, how it should be carried out, whom it ought to enrol, what role each member of the team should perform in relation to the others, and what kinds of results should emerge from it. There ought to be a scientific experiment. The experiment should take place in a laboratory. It will, most likely, involve a scanner. (Increasingly, in our experience, fMRI is regarded as the default option, though positron

DOI: 10.1057/9781137407962.0008

emission tomography (PET), electroencephalography (EEG), and other technologies are of course also possible.) The cognitive neuroscientist should be on hand to conduct the experiment and process the data; the psychologist should take charge of fine-tuning the protocol (sometimes the neuroscientist and the cognitive psychologist are subsumed within one person); the bioethicist should be there to soothe our consciences about any ethical implications of the study; the social scientist should be there to help assess the suitability of the sample and to comment on the generalizability of the findings; the philosopher should be there to ensure rigorous parsing and application of constructs (and to make the tea). The most important data to emerge are those produced through the coming together of the human experimental subject(s) and the scanner; these should be published in a neuroscientific journal (though ancillary publications that address other disciplines' concerns are of course welcomed).

In short: what emerges here is a spatial imaginary centred on the model of a multi- (rather than inter-) disciplinary mix, a mix that will establish, it is hoped, a methodological and conceptual 'layer cake'. (We are employing here the usual distinction between the multi-disciplinary, in which disciplines line up alongside one another, from the interdisciplinary, which usually carries some commitment towards creating emergent, and novel forms of knowledge different from those contained within any one discipline.) Within this layer cake, each disciplinary layer has dominion over a particular kind of expertise, particular methods, and particular objects of knowledge. You can see this play out in numerous published interdisciplinary books and studies that address the mind and brain (see e.g. Goldman 2006; Slaby and Gallagher 2015). Joseph Dumit, we should note, has provided a powerful analysis of how cognitive psychology was brought into contact with PET to produce the interdisciplinary layer cake that became the foundation of the interdisciplinary field of cognitive neuroscience (Dumit 2004). We should not be unduly surprised, therefore, that the layer cake functions as the buttressing logic for other interdisciplinary endeavours involving the brain and mind.

There are a few examples that depart from the layer cake genre. Roepstorff and Frith, for example, in elaborating a model of experimental anthropology 'as a method, as an object of study and as a research aesthetic', argue that joint engagement (*doing things together*) in research projects across the disciplines leads to the need for researchers of all stripes then to 'be sensitive both to the type of facts and the types of contexts produced by going experimental' (Roepstorff and Frith 2012,

DOI: 10.1057/9781137407962.0008

108). The dominance of the layer cake model, however, means that the methods and technologies of cognitive neuroscience tend to be endowed with a particular luminosity and generativity. *And we emphasize that it is often social scientists and humanities scholars, rather than neuroscientists themselves, who manifest the greatest enthusiasm in doing so.* In short, it is the brain scanning technology (of whatever kind) that ends up being granted the most substantial epistemological value (which nicely sits alongside its substantial economic weight). Experts from other disciplines can help to fine-tune, interpret, or contextualize what goes into it, and what comes out of it, but the work that the scanner does is where the real action is.

Such a model tends, at the same time, to embed a particular temporality at the heart of interdisciplinary labours in this arena. As soon as the cognitive neuroscientific fMRI study is installed as the groundwork of the collaboration, all are constrained by two particular timelines. First: when is the scanner available? (This is *always* a vexed question.) Second: how lengthy will the period of recruitment need to be to find people to insert into the scanner? The difficulty with this model is that its spatial and temporal characteristics occlude the multiple other modes through which collaborations might unfold, and through which interventions – into existing literatures, and into the worlds of experimentation and investigation – might take place. What would it mean to conduct an interdisciplinary experiment that did not orient itself around the temporal logic of scanner availability? What if the scanner had to wait, instead, on the very different – but no less fraught – timekeeping that is inherent to the ethnographic method? What if an interdisciplinary workshop, which had been initially planned so as to fine-tune the constructs under investigation in the forthcoming neuroimaging study, ended up determining that a neuroimaging experiment were not necessarily the most appropriate kind of experimental procedure to engage in? What if philosophers were freed up – and freed themselves up – to do more than maintain the conceptual rigour of psychological constructs? (For one example of this, see Haueis 2014.)

Good fences make good neighbours

"No: I don't agree with your account of the permeability of disciplines, one to the other, at all. I do think that good fences make good neighbours."

DOI: 10.1057/9781137407962.0008

Both of us were at the workshop at which a highly regarded interdisciplinary researcher conveyed this strong account of appropriate interdisciplinary practice – one that defended disciplinary turfs and disciplinary expertise. The sentence above was spoken after one of us (FC) had countered what she interpreted as the academic's territorialized landscape of interdisciplinarity with a question about the untoward relationalities unfurled by postcolonial studies – as well as by other interdisciplinary theoretical domains that have been committed to queering the pitch of orthodox histories and geographies. In many ways, we understood this researcher's response. In calling for interdisciplinarity, no one wants to be misunderstood as championing sloppiness, and few, we imagine, want to be interpellated as the inevitable jack of all trades and master of none. We certainly would not want to find ourselves endorsing, say, an analytical philosopher who planned to get by in an interdisciplinary project, untrained, as a sociologist; we do not wish to champion an anthropologist who imagines she can, in a trice, become a conceptual artist. But in this chapter we want, nonetheless, to challenge the spatial logic of fences and neighbours – and the specific forms of territory it brings into being. Here is discipline thought through the figure of the happy householder – willing to reach over the fence, for sure, but still very keen to maintain a proper sense of where the boundaries lie. Indeed, there is an important claim embedded in this metaphor (and one hears it all the time) of good fences, insofar as it dramatizes what is still sometimes an unquestioned assumption about the primacy of the private space of disciplinary training.

Whatever our – and your – feelings about private property might be, it strikes us that there is a pernicious notion, embedded here, that maps intellectual inquiry on to the taken-for-granted boundaries of relationships between public and private space. (In this regard, we find it intriguing that many writings that address cross-disciplinarity employ language that conjures private property relations. We might turn, for example, to the philosopher Brian Massumi, who discusses the 'poaching' of a scientific concept (which, moreover, on his account, does not result in 'prevent[ing] it from continuing to function in its *home* environment', and who maintains that if he 'were a concept, [he] could emigrate *and* stay behind in [his] home country' [italics in original] (Massumi 2002, 21)); or to Thomas Osborne, who describes interdisciplinary movements via languages of poaching and trespass (Osborne 2013).) What would change, for the kinds of projects that we are trying to bring into

DOI: 10.105/9781137407962.0008

being, if we were to think though very different accounts of property, of home, of migration, of arrangement, and of distinction? What if we were to recall, for example, the commons that preceded those strong fences? What if we were to turn to forms of community relation, and of being-in-common, that refused – for good and for ill – the always-assumed bourgeois propriety of *neighbourliness*?

After fiefdom

In her analysis of the intellectual terrain marked out by the term 'American Studies', literary studies scholar Wai Chee Dimock demonstrates how a 'fiefdom' has been drawn under the first half of that term, such that the founding adjective *American* comes to '[govern] the domain of inquiry we construct, the range of questions we entertain, the kind of evidence we take as significant' (Dimock 2001, 755). Does not the adjective 'interdisciplinary' do the same kind of demarcation work? Consider how that term, for example, constitutes itself as a place of intensity and the site of boundary transgression; consider also how it sets out a specific range of allowable – and not allowable – modes of investigation; and how it, in so doing, in fact occludes the congealed, compacted 'interdisciplinary' peregrinations of those 'disciplines' from which it apparently draws. For, as Philippe Fontaine reminds us, the dominance of the image of 'two cultures' (sciences and humanities), marked by fences and boundary-points, has tended to elide the distinctive history of the social sciences as a particular culture – and, in particular, the development of a post-war social scientific culture that was intensely 'cross-disciplinary' in both its intentions and its practices (2015, 2; see also other essays in that special issue of *Journal of the History of the Behavioral Sciences*). As Fitzgerald, Rose, and Singh (forthcoming) have argued elsewhere, there is a far more entangled palette of relationships between, say, psychiatry and sociology, or between psychology and political science, than those imagined in orthodox accounts of ordered interdisciplinary exchange. Andrew Pickering, similarly, has pointed out that cybernetics, far from simply combining existing disciplines, 'amounted to the explosion of a nonmodern ontological stance across, and beyond, the disciplinary map' (Pickering 2013, 217).

How might such insights help us to rethink the spatial and temporal commitments of interdisciplinarity (as well as those of 'disciplinarity'

DOI: 10.1057/9781137407962.0008

on which they are founded)? Can we, as Dimock suggests in another context, 'draw a different input map of the world' (2008, 29)? Elsewhere, we have proposed a rethinking of the interdisciplinary scene through a logic of 'experimental entanglement' – in an attempt to gesture at our shared realization that working across the social sciences, neurosciences, and humanities was not at all about figuring out how to move fences, or how to work across them; instead it was about recognizing how tangled were the roots into which those stakes were driven into in the first place (Fitzgerald and Callard 2015). In advancing the spatial dimensions of that conceptual move, we offer, below, four additional terms that help us to think about the patterning and arrangements of interdisciplinary entanglements. What we hope is that these might move all of our imaginaries away from that of the layer cake, or that they might spark, in some readers, new and allied terms of their own.

Matrices

The spatial logics that underpin the management of interdisciplinary projects tend to fall, we believe, into two, not mutually exclusive, categories: (1) a dominant principal investigator, looking down upon all the disciplinary ranks; and (2) fantasized – and ever thwarted – parity across these ranks. Both logics envisage interdisciplinarity through the efficient arrangement of different-but-equal silos – to use the management *cliché*. A matrix, by contrast, opens up a very different kind of spatial and temporal imaginary – one that attends more closely to the 'organizational physiology' of the project, to use Bartlett and Ghoshal's (1990) evocative term. The term matrix carries long histories. Alongside its use as a designator of the womb, it denotes the environment in which something is created or developed; it is also variously employed within biology, pharmacology, mathematics, business, sociology, and political theory. What draws us, then, to this term, is its history of promiscuous movement across terrains of expertise and interest, and the manner in which it draws attention to the multiple ways in which to understand the processes and pressures of connection, support, embedding, binding, and generation.

In the history of organizational design, matrix structures were championed, against the bureaucratized hierarchy of the post-war years, as ways of putting things and people together, around specific questions, with an attention to the quality of *lateral* relations – pointing out that the unidirectional flow of information 'up' to a single manager of a

DOI: 10.105/9781137407962.0008

single department stymies both communication and creativity (see e.g. Sayles 1976). If we replace the 'manager' with the 'disciplinary expert', the power of the matrix for rethinking logics of collaboration becomes clear. And we need not seek inspiration only in the management literature: the complex and variable 'meshwork' of proteins that make up the extracellular matrix of animal tissue was once thought to be an 'inert scaffold', but is now thought to play 'a far more active and complex role in regulating the behaviour of the cells that contact it, influencing their survival, development, migration, proliferation, shape and function' (Alberts et al. 2002). It is worth thinking further about how working with and through matrices might afford new means through which collaborative interdisciplinary projects and relations might be set into motion. One example, here, is Hubbub, though Hubbub is far from being the only place that we could turn. Hubbub's Core Group (the principal investigator and co-investigators of the research project) have attempted precisely to attend to this pliable meshwork, much more than the cells – or silos – themselves. Collaborators, from whichever discipline, are encouraged to self-organize as they like, and communicate amongst themselves; disciplinary experts neither form teams around projects, nor tend to act as gateways to the joining of projects. We would certainly not want to imply that the project exists without checkpoints in some magical, frictionless space: we are sure that many collaborators could enumerate multiple ways in which they are baulked from moving, playing and binding. But we still contend that what is most at stake, around any individual project within Hubbub, is not the specific expertise a person 'brings', but rather her capacity to fold into, and expand, a matrix that is developing around a particular question.

Topologies

Across the sciences, social sciences, and humanities, the topological has become, in recent decades, a particularly resonant mode through which to map the enfolding relations that enjoin entities and constitute dynamics. Researchers in this mode draw upon topological theories, as they have emerged in the mathematics of continuous space, to think more broadly about the ways in which (as a series of events on 'topology' as Tate Modern put it) 'static ideas of space as a container [might be] replaced by understandings of movement-space, of multiplicity, differentiation and exclusive inclusion that in turn have led to new ideas of power, subjectivity, and creativity' (Tate 2012). As Celia Lury

DOI: 10.1057/9781137407962.0008

and colleagues have argued, 'topology is now *emergent* in the practices of ordering, modelling, networking and mapping that co-constitute culture, technology and science' (Lury, Parisi, and Terranova 2012, 5; our italics). The language of topology, as Martin and Secor have analysed, is one full of 'flows, deformations, twists, folds, torsions, severations, and cuts' – and thereby well positioned to be variously employed 'as a metaphor, a heuristic device, an analytical approach, a figure, and an ontological relationship' (Martin and Secor 2014, 421). We cannot but gesture here to the genealogies and theorizations of topology – which have dense histories in scientific, philosophical, social scientific, and psychoanalytic literatures.

We worry, then, that our invocation of the topological will function simply as yet more adulation for one of the terms *du jour*. But if we persist in mentioning topology, it is because the term points to the need to attend closely to how one registers, analyses, and represents the dynamics, connections, breaks and transformations to which entities captured through a language of 'the topological' are subject. Those entities might be collaborative groups, experimental situations, or biosocial entities. What has been vital to this topological turn is attention to how nodes and edges are being defined: topological analyses are built around nodes and those connections that enjoin them. One way to think about this is to imagine how things might shift if different objects or technologies were set to fold into one another within interdisciplinary space – or if we brought to visibility often ignored nodes that might be present within the collaborative groups, experimental situations or biosocial entities under investigation. (One interesting example here is the 'multispecies network analysis' conducted by Michael Pettit and colleagues to understand historical relations between scientists, their preferred experimental animals, and institutions during inter-war research on sexual behaviour, and hence to demonstrate the often unacknowledged importance of particular laboratory animals in the constitution of distinct disciplinary and institutional cultures (Pettit, Serykh, and Green 2015).) We are reminded, here, of some of the most imaginative interdisciplinary neuroscientific studies that have been conducted within the laboratory of Andreas Roepstorff at Aarhus University (a sometime collaborator of ours) – in which the edges of anthropological and neurobiological accounts of intersubjectivity are rendered continuous, with intellect and attention coming to rest on the forms of enjambment that might run them together (see e.g. Xygalatas et al. 2011). What distinguishes the

DOI: 10.105/9781137407962.0008

intensely interdisciplinary work of Roepstorff and his collaborators is precisely this attention to the space of continuity, and to the forms of nodularity and edgework (both inside and outside the scanner) through which those continuities are made empirically visible.

Incorporations

Psychoanalysis proposes very different accounts of relationality, sociality, and negativity from many of those found within social and cultural theory. We could not be further from a world of happy zones of neighbourly exchange (or even from a world of carefully plotted poaching and trespass). What would it mean to think interdisciplinary spatialities and temporalities through, and with, the relationalities offered by Freud (or by many of those who followed him), instead of with the sanitized models of the 'inter-' that have colonized many formal and informal accounts of interdisciplinarity? For Freud, for example, incorporation marked the primitive wish to unite with, identify with, or cannibalistically annihilate an object. Within psychoanalysis more broadly, incorporation – theorized as a mode of ferocious identification – is one of the most foundational kinds of relationality (Laplanche and Pontalis 1968). It is this dynamic of ferocity and pleasure that distinguishes the spatial mode of incorporation. It is also a relational logic that is frequently at play within interdisciplinary projects, though its pleasures (and its dangers) are rarely acknowledged. Such a relational logic makes clear the indispensability of negativity in *any* account of relationality. Such indispensability has been perhaps made most clear by a dense braid of cultural-theoretical work in the humanities, which has been indebted both to Freud and to the foundational insights of queer theory (e.g. Edelman 2004). While much of this work has been quickly designated as 'anti-social', we are more interested in how it deforms our usual understandings of social relations. As Elizabeth Wilson has argued:

> negativity is intrinsic (rather than antagonistic) to sociality and subjectivity..., and this makes a world of difference politically. This queer work isn't antisocial at all; rather, it wants to build theories that can stomach the fundamental involvement of negativity in sociality and subjectivity. (Wilson 2015, 6)

We have been keen in our research not to extrude negative, ferocious, and corrosive forms of relation and of sociality. (Outside of our empirical research within the interdisciplinary neuroscience–social science domain, one of us (FC) has been particularly interested in how these

DOI: 10.105/9781137407962.0008

problematics are recognized or ignored in the course of interdisciplinary 'transfers' of terms and knowledges, for example: in the taming of psycho-analysis within geography (Callard 2003); in the use of scientific models of affect within the humanities and social sciences (Papoulias and Callard 2010); or in the strange disavowal of Freud's uncanny relationalities in the nascent field of neuropsychoanalysis (Papoulias and Callard 2012).) We are also interested in our own desires for identification with the biologi-cal – desires whose reasoned articulation (and we are sometimes not even capable of such articulation) always leaves us slightly unfulfilled.

Processes such as incorporation push us, in turn, to acknowledge how our collaborations do not bring us together as rational economic actors, across (what are thought to be) disciplinary lines, engaging in friendly exchange with our neighbours. We – and 'we' is employed broadly, here – are also propelled by preconscious and unconscious acts of ferocious identification with, ambivalence regarding, and envy of the other. The question then is: what kind of organizational and spatial logics might emerge from, or at least take account of, such unruly forms of relation? Or does this term remind us, rather, that there are (infantile, primitive) desires for proximity and ingestion that it might be as well to sate as to understand? How would our interactions with our collaborators change if we understood ourselves all to be variously constituted through and by ambivalence, envy, and ferocious acts of identification?

Laboratories

At least since the early work of Bruno Latour and Steve Woolgar (1986), the laboratory – as a physical space, a set of procedures, and an arrange-ment of people and things – has been the site of intense interest within the history of science, and science and technology studies. The labora-tory, as Steven Shapin and Simon Schaffer point out in their seminal account of the debate between Boyle and Hobbes (1989), emerged in the seventeenth century as a space of constrained tinkering, witnessing, and demonstrating; it has a specific history within the natural sciences that is not only much less obvious or necessary than is often imagined, but is a good deal less innocent too (Haraway 1997). Laboratory is a capa-cious term, holding together not only a space of demonstration (e.g. the MRI suite) but also a norm of investigation (a laboratory science), as well as a highly contingent group (such as 'my lab') bound together around particular questions (see also Knorr Cetina 1992). But it is the choreography holding these different senses of laboratory together

DOI: 10.1057/9781137407962.0008

that captures our attention here: a laboratory calls a group together; it directs attention to careful arrangements of humans and non-humans that make up a particular laboratory assemblage; and it sets out norms, within such an assemblage, for who must demonstrate, and who must witness, and from where they must do it in either case. Additionally, laboratories, as the historian of science Hans-Jörg Rheinberger has argued, pose the question of how experimental knowledge is captured through various modes of writing, tracing, and recording: '[r]eduction to a surface facilitates exploration of new ways of ordering and arranging data: sequential events can be presented in synchronic form'. Rheinberger asks, furthermore, whether there might be ' "collective" equivalents of such individual forms of scientific note-taking and write-ups', such that one might discern collaborative graphic traces that might tell us not only about the cultures of a particular laboratory, but might provoke new research questions (Rheinberger 2010, 251). What might this mean for practices of collaborative interdisciplinarity across the neurosciences, social sciences, and humanities? (We are particularly gripped by this question, given that we are currently collaborating with many researchers from the humanities and the arts, for whom graphic traces are central to their own experimental practices.)

Lately, such a choreography has been invoked by a range of interdisciplinary centres, such as the MIT Media Lab, the Urban Laboratory at University College London, or the Culture Lab at Newcastle University. One of us (DF) worked on a project that calls itself an 'urban brain lab', where the word is invoked precisely to associate with a particular kind of, and normative commitment to, proximity with others and their work – *viz.* a cathexis of people, disciplines, and interests in which the arrangement of those elements is prioritized above each individual's intellectual histories. One might see similar commitment in the various groupings that have described themselves as 'collaboratories' (see e.g. Collier n.d.). If 'laboratory' is a troubled term for many social scientists, it is not a ludicrous one. Spatially and temporally, one of its greatest advantages is that it moves us beyond many of the fantasies that many social scientists orient themselves towards (such as the 'the interpretive and authorial virtuosity of an individual', as Andrew Lakoff and his colleagues have argued (Lakoff, Collier, and Rabinow 2006, 5)). What would it meant to reimagine ourselves as co-workers experimenting and scribbling in a laboratory, rather than neighbours talking over a fence?

DOI: 10.1057/9781137407962.0008

Into the void

> *The atmosphere was one of a strained energetics: all of us, delegates at an inter-disciplinary workshop, were wanting – in fact, longing – to find points of connec-tion and reassurance across what might have been seen as yawning disciplinary divides. Our expertise stretched from early medieval history, to early modern history, to cognitive psychology, to medical humanities, to geography. Each of us, in the course of the workshop, had been plunged, during talks, into the strange alterity of worlds and modes of academic presentation very different from our own; many in the room had discerned wonderful and startling connections between accounts of people's sensory perceptions in different time periods, and current models in cognitive psychology and cognitive neuroscience to investigate those phenomena. Delegates frequently used phrases such as 'this reminds me of something from my own field'; 'this resonates with a concept from my discipline'; 'it seems to be the same formulation'. Felicity began to wonder if we weren't all working rather too hard, and if there might not be something to be said, ulti-mately, for sometimes* not *connecting.*

In this chapter, we have worked with and through some of the spatio-temporal imaginaries through which researchers might plot as well as practise interdisciplinary research. We have used four terms (which are also, and variously, phenomena, constructs, abstractions, and metaphori-cal resources) to open up ways of conceptualizing the spatial organization of interdisciplinarity that push beyond those indebted to particular ways of carving territory and terrain, and that centre on producing connec-tion, entanglement, and ingestion in the collaborative sphere.

Yet one important problem remains. In the current impetus towards collaboration, there is, we suggest, an implicit normative assumption of *connection* itself, and indeed of relationality as such. What happens to collaboration when connection is impossible to refuse? What becomes of those ontological and epistemological voids – which is to say, those spaces and temporalities that cannot be produced or even glimpsed within the current dispensation? Paul Harrison has argued, in response to the inter-est across a number of disciplines in 'relation' and 'relationality' (and here our earlier invocations of matrices and topologies are two such instances), that the question of the non-relational is at threat of occlusion:

> it seems to me that in the proliferation of biophilosophy, the unstoppable materialisation of actor networks and constructivist totalisations of the social

DOI: 10.105/9781137407962.0008

or the cultural, few have been asking about breaks and gaps, interruptions and intervals, caesuras and tears. (Harrison 2007, 592)

For Harrison, much more work is required to think through what is 'meant by the term "relation"' if we are not simply to produce a 'quantitatively expanded sociospatial imaginary rather than a shift towards the appreciation of intervallic topologies, complex figures, and diverse phrases and regimens' (Harrison 2007, 590). Consider, in this respect, the nascent interdisciplinary field of neuropsychoanalysis (Panksepp and Solms 2011). That field has founded itself on the conviction that it is possible to bring together psychoanalysis, (certain kinds of cognitive and affective) neuroscience, and evolutionary biology. But what gets missed, in such an insistence, are precisely the things that might not go together. Consider, for example, against that insistence, Jean Laplanche's readings of Freud (e.g. Laplanche 1989), which force to the surface the impossibility of making Freud's account 'consonant with a model of the organism that is centred around adaptive need' (Papoulias and Callard 2012, 211). We retain an anxiety that our focus on spatial logics of collaboration is already a refusal of this impossibility. We want to learn to collaborate in a world that is constituted as much through voids and non-relation as through contact and relation.

Notes & Queries: 5

Q: What kinds of people do I need for an interdisciplinary project involving the neurosciences, social sciences (and, perhaps, the humanities)? How do I arrange them?

A: This is a complex question – and one that opens in multiple directions, depending on the kind of phenomena you want to investigate, and the kinds of research you are interested in conducting. We wouldn't for a moment want to imply that one can specify in advance the kinds of people one would need without attending to the particularities of a potential project. What we would say, however – and this is in the interests of departing from the 'layer cake' model we have described in this chapter – is that it's worth thinking carefully before you decide you 'need' a psychologist, or an anthropologist, or a sociologist, or a cognitive neuroscientist, or a clinical researcher to make your interdisciplinary project work. It

DOI: 10.1057/9781137407962.0008

might be helpful to explore the function that this initially perceived 'need' is serving and to disarticulate expertise in particular methods (performing statistical regressions; translating medieval Latin texts) from expertise in a discipline. There is also the important question of how appropriate expertise to take part in an interdisciplinary project does not necessarily map neatly on to seniority.

In many of the interdisciplinary projects in which we have been involved, we have been struck by: (1) what emerges – what topological relations unfold – from having people in the room with expertise in disciplines not commonly regarded as central to interdisciplinary neuroscientific projects (e.g. a poet, a medieval historian, a composer); (2) the torqueing of various disciplinary or discursive assumptions when the project includes people with varied disciplinary trainings (e.g. we are thinking of one of our collaborators who has expertise in computer science, anthropology, science and technology studies, and the history of science).

DOI: 10.1057/9781137407962.0008

6

Against Reciprocity: Dynamics of Power in Interdisciplinary Spaces

Abstract: *All too often, 'reciprocity' emerges as the (imagined) organizing logic of interdisciplinary collaboration – with collaborators invited to forms of mutuality, fair exchange, and so on. In this chapter, we show what is missing from this analysis, which is any account of power. The chapter thus takes up an analysis of how power works in an interdisciplinary space – setting out, in particular, some of the different financial, epistemic, and cultural resources that belong to different disciplines. But if the chapter sets itself against one fantasy (fair exchange), it also wants to dispel another – and this is the fantasy of power confronted by the frankly-spoken truth. The chapter argues instead for what it might mean to think interdisciplinary collaboration as a practice of subjugation, which different collaborators may just have to learn to live with.*

Keywords: collaboration; interdisciplinarity; power; subjugation; trading zones

Callard, Felicity and Des Fitzgerald. *Rethinking Interdisciplinarity across the Social Sciences and Neurosciences.* Basingstoke: Palgrave Macmillan, 2015. DOI: 10.1057/9781137407962.0009.

 DOI: 10.1057/9781137407962.0009

Introduction

The familiar register of exhortations to interdisciplinarity – mutuality! reciprocity! exchange! – is one that assumes that differentials of power do not exist. And yet, for many people from the humanities and social sciences – and we are thinking quite beyond our own collaborations here – experiencing one's role in a collaboration with life scientists as a relatively powerless one undercuts these kinds of exhortations. Go to the bar at any science and technology studies conference, and it won't take too many drinks before social scientists start telling you about how their research is often understood as 'public engagement'; how they consistently have to justify their expertise to their collaborators; how they have to translate (or sometimes give up on) their conceptual language in a way that is not always reciprocated, and so on. This doesn't mean that life scientists in collaborations are especially power-hungry; or that they behave badly (no doubt most would be surprised and taken aback to learn that their collaborators would narrate their experience in such ways). But it *is* to say that when a group of people collaborate within institutional structures that end up placing the more highly valued epistemological frameworks, as well as financial resources, largely on one side, then asymmetries result.

Even among – and perhaps especially among – the most well-meaning people, such asymmetries can produce some unlovely relations. It is important to note that such relations are rarely, if ever, explicitly endorsed by collaborating life scientists, and life scientists themselves often do not gain from them. Indeed, to the extent that interdisciplinary asymmetries of power can produce silences and absences, there is a significant risk that they reduce the space for the complex collaborative entanglements that motivate many scientific collaborators in the first place. Perhaps more importantly, and this is perhaps not always so visible to collaborators, even if natural scientists in particular collaborations may appear to hold all the power, those scientists *themselves* are subject to precisely the same asymmetries, when they reenter a larger prestige economy that might mark their collaborations with social scientists or humanities scholars as decidedly low-value contributions. And this is to say nothing of the way that natural scientists may experience a more subtle asymmetry, as they get pinioned by the philosopher's or literary theorist's rhetorical monopoly on, and their own explicit exclusion from, what it means to think 'critically'. (Indeed, we have lost track of the number of times we

DOI: 10.105/9781137407962.0009

have heard humanities scholars and interpretive social scientists lament the naivety of scientists for having the temerity to proceed as if the world were real, or for going ahead with experiments that are patently 'reductionistic' of the phenomena they are studying, as though the scientists haven't thought long and hard about which kinds of reduction might be most potent in the particular experimental situation in which they find themselves.) It is true that we are two social scientists who have, at times, found ourselves on the wrong end of such relations, and we will not deny that this chapter is significantly motivated by our own desires to understand and think those relations as *we* have felt them. Still, even as we emphasize the partiality of our account, we insist that such an interpretive labour is vital for the collaborating natural scientist too.

In what follows, then, we think through relations of power in interdisciplinary research projects that bring the biosciences and the social sciences into intimacy with one another. We will be concerned not so much with providing a rich sociological account of how power operates in collaborative projects, but, rather, with the ways in which significantly interdisciplinary research in those spaces is *produced through* structures of power that position different people, and objects, and ideas, in very specific ways. At the heart of the chapter is an attempt to show that interdisciplinarity is entangled in much thicker structures of power than either its promoters or its practitioners are willing to recognize. We hope that that it is clear, already, that what follows is not a screed about the fantastic power of neuroscience. (Nor do we want to be misread as wilfully ignoring the multiple and diverse instances of generosity, and laborious work on our behalf, that our collaborators have shown towards us.) Even as we work through our *own*, often fraught, relationship with what we experience as collaborative asymmetry (and we have *only* this to work through), the chapter remains motivated by a distinctly ambivalent relationship both to how power operates (we do not describe, here, a simple pinioning of one 'side' by another), and to what it might make possible. This final point guides the second half of the chapter: here, we are going to claim that interdisciplinary collaborators need to give up not only the official fantasy of 'mutuality', but also on that fantasy's self-consciously critical mirror-image, *viz.* the idea that relations of power need either to be *overcome* or at least *faced up to* through reinvigorated forms of transparent dialogue, mutual respect, frank talking, and manifestations of emotions appropriate to the situation, such as anger (e.g. see Rabinow 2009). In what follows, we are going to reach towards a less comfortable

DOI: 10.1057/9781137407962.0009

conclusion: oftentimes, we suggest, the labour of collaboration is less a task of learning to speak up for yourself – in the service, say, of 'achieving a more just recognition [for one's] substantial efforts and contributions' as social scientists or humanities scholars (Rabinow 2009, 318) – and rather more a labour of adjusting to, precariously acquiescing to, and, on occasion, becoming curiously attached to, states of subjugation.

We offer one final disclaimer before proceeding: at least since the work of Michel Foucault (e.g. Foucault 1982), and probably indeed going back to the writing of Max Weber (see e.g. Wallimann, Tatsis, and Zito 1977), power has been a central concept – one might say a 'master concept' – of the interpretive social sciences (as well as significant parts of the humanities). When we talk about power in this chapter, we commonly use it in the more commonsensical Weberian sense (i.e. as the ability 'to secure one's own ends' in a social relationship (Wallimann, Tatsis, and Zito 1977, 231)). But occasionally, too, we invoke the term in Foucault's sense (i.e. as a technique that 'categorizes the individual, marks him by his own individuality ... [and] imposes a law of truth on him which he must recognize' (Foucault 1982, 781)). The chapter is undoubtedly inflected, too, by other theoretical and philosophical interventions on power and subjugation that work to understand how it is that 'the subject is the kind of being who can be exploited, who is, by virtue of its own formation, vulnerable to subjugation' (Butler 1997, 20). Again: we are indebted to accounts of subjecthood and to relationality in which exposure to and entanglement with power is a deeply ambivalent process, one in which what is unbearable can also be the site of hope and strange attachments (see e.g. Berlant and Edelman 2014).

Such theoretical armature is, probably, of little concern to those readers more preoccupied with our accounts of what it's like to live in these interdisciplinary spaces. We mention these lineages, however, to alert those who *are* interested to the fact that we have thought long and hard about subjugation both inside and outside the interdisciplinary settings that are our specific focus here. We want to forestall a response that we commonly receive to our invocations of subjugation, *viz.* being lambasted for our political pusillanimity and/or for our unhappy turning away from 'the demands of the day' (e.g. Stavrianakis et al. 2014). By claiming a space for subjugation, we are neither jettisoning the importance of anger, nor the need to acknowledge that social relations of collaboration are, on occasion, intolerable and irreparable. But we contest a logic in which social scientists and humanities scholars should, in the face of

DOI: 10.1057/9781137407962.0009

such relations, remain tethered to a fantasied longing for recognition, or for an endorsement of their own value within those collaborations.

Mutual intellectual and professional respect

Rhetorics of reciprocation and mutuality suffuse the 'grey' literature on interdisciplinarity. Here, for example, is the description of an inter-disciplinary funding programme, 'Science in Culture', run by the UK's Arts and Humanities Research Council (AHRC): the Science in Culture theme 'aims to develop the reciprocal relationship between the sciences on the one hand, and arts and humanities on the other'; through such reciprocal relationships, the theme will 'encourage mutual exchanges between the sciences and the arts and humanities that offer scope for developing new areas of research, methodologies, research frameworks styles of thinking and/or ways of working across the disciplines' (Arts & Humanities Research Council 2015). Or consider this promotional mate-rial for a conference on interdisciplinarity at Durham University: 'By exchanging knowledges interdisciplinary collaboration has the potential to generate new thinking and transform the way that participants think about their own work. This can be tremendously exciting and reward-ing' (Durham University n.d.). Or take this statement from the 'Vilnius Declaration' on the role of the social sciences and humanities ('SSH') in the European Union's Horizon 2020 research funding programme:

> Solving the most pressing societal challenges requires the appropriate inclu-sion of SSH. This can only succeed on a basis of mutual intellectual and profes-sional respect and in genuine partnership. Efficient integration will require novel ways of defining research problems, aligned with an appropriate array of interdisciplinary methods and theoretical approaches. SSH approaches continue to foster practical applications that enhance the effectiveness of technical solutions. (Mayer, König, and Nowotny 2013, 26)

Integration. Mutuality. Reciprocation. Rewarding exchange. Shared solutions. Such is the terminology through which both the bureaucratic and intellectual imaginaries of interdisciplinary research take shape. There is a very particular idea of interdisciplinary *exchange* embedded in this language: one in which actors from different disciplines, if they are not exactly (or not quite yet) trading and exchanging their knowledge in settings characterized by mutual respect and reciprocation, then at least

DOI: 10.1057/9781137407962.009

this is something they're aiming for. As the organizers of the Vilnius conference (the event that produced the 'Vilnius Declaration', cited above) put it:

> the SSH community should be alerted to reflect on how to deal more actively with the opportunities that the shifting framework conditions of Horizon 2020 offer to them, instead of complaining about losing their stakes. .... Only through a mutual and open discussion how to shape and practically apply the 'integrative approach' could [this conference] be made to work in earnest. (Mayer, König, and Nowotny 2013, 16)

But there is surely more going on, here, than the optimism we might see undergirding this desire. The Vilnius Conference was organized precisely because the European Union, in putting together its eighth Framework Programme for research funding, favoured an 'integrative' interdisciplinary approach, which many saw as a diminution of the role of the social sciences and humanities. In other words, the conference came at the foot of a series of 'interdisciplinary' developments that served very precisely to demonstrate how *marginal* these disciplines sometimes are to the intentions of powerful actors. And yet still the hope – of a 'mutual and open discussion' – remains.

Fantasies of power

What is little mentioned across these bureaucratic and public-facing formulations is how interdisciplinary collaborations are structured through very different adjudications of epistemic authority (but see the contribution of Ulrike Felt in Mayer, Konig, and Nowotny 2013, 57) – or that, within and beyond particular projects, different actors have access to very different pots of money; that their practices of writing are differently legible, that they are differentially supported by governments and private foundations; that their views carry differential weights within policy communities, and so on.

Things look a little different if one turns to the scholarly literature. In an analysis of an emergent interdisciplinary field crossing economics and geography, for example, geographer Erica Schoenberger worries about how historically nuanced concepts and methods that are central to her own discipline are disregarded in a 'disciplinary imperialism': the new endeavour 'exclude[s] social conflict and power relations, which are both

DOI: 10.105/9781137407962.0009

mathematically and ideologically inconvenient...*geography* has been excised from an activity that nonetheless calls itself the new economic geography' (Schoenberger 2001, 378). And it is forms of 'social power' – which is to say, in this case, powerful institutions (Harvard and MIT) and disciplines (economics) – that make the difference. Sharachchandra Lélé and Richard Norgaard, drawing on their work in interdisciplinary climate-change projects, put the situation even more starkly: 'there are', they point out, 'significant differences in the manner in which society treats the social and natural sciences...Naturally, the social sciences are seen as irrelevant, boring, and nonrigorous....' They go on:

> the social scientists, because they purportedly were not good enough to get into the 'science stream', are often in awe of the natural sciences. The belief of the superiority of the natural scientists is so deep-rooted that whenever social problems have the slightest technical dimension, politicians have tradition-ally called on only technicians – the natural scientists – to help solve them. (Lélé and Norgaard 2005, 971–972)

Not only do social scientists get side-lined in such projects, on Lélé and Norgaard's account, but natural scientists are asked to fill the breach: 'Charged with providing policy recommendations, [natural scientists] have to make judgments about how society works. They do not have adequate training to do this, but they are perhaps emboldened to do so by their position and are likely to adopt simplistic models of social dynamics' (Lélé and Norgaard 2005, 970).

In one empirical analysis of an interdisciplinary sustainability project, Susan Gardner shows how attention to status and hierarchy ran through the project – with her social science interlocutors giving their answers through 'nervous laughter' versus what Gradner describes as the more self-confident responses of the natural scientists. 'I have some difficulty seeing some of the value of some of the social sciences', one of the natu-ral scientists tells Gardner: 'I have sat through a number of lectures that some of the social science people have given and walked away wondering what the point was' (Gardner 2012, 248). Another tells Gardener that the social scientists on the project are pretty 'squishy' – ' "Where were the hypotheses? How much data were gathered? Where are the statistics?" ' (Gardner 2012, 248).

To be sure, this is a one-sided account: even if it is not obvious in the literature we have presented above, we have no difficulty in believing (indeed, are assured by our scientist collaborators that it is the case)

DOI: 10.1057/9781137407962.0009

that collaborating life scientists, too, experience such asymmetries. This occurs both within individual collaborations (one can well imagine the humanist's equivalent of 'Where were the hypotheses?') and beyond them: to collaborate with people who might be a bit 'squishy', after all, is unlikely to represent much a grab for the garlands and esteem of your scientific peers. But rather than cataloguing this back and forth, what we want to do here is undercut the fantasy that might follow on from *both* sets of complaints. This is the fantasy of power confronted. For Lélé and Norgaard, for example, the key to high-quality interdisciplinary practice is researchers throwing into question the barriers that generate these biases: 'contrary to their disciplinary training', they argue,

> participants [in interdisciplinary projects] need to be self-reflective about the value judgments embedded in their choice of variables and models, willing to give respect to and also learn more about the 'other', and able to work with new models and taxonomies used by others. (Lélé and Norgaard 2005, 975)

For Schoenberger, geography should revert to its own internal interdisciplinarity (here geography is in a relatively unusual position, we would say), or it could go looking for more interesting economists to talk to (Schoenberger 2001, 379–380). For Bronislaw Szerszynski and Maialen Galarraga, who are especially interested in the case of geo-engineering, the task of social scientists in these situations is to 'expose assumptions, bring out the multiplicity and incommensurability of different views and ontologies, and keep problem definitions open' – thus producing 'greater diversity and reflexivity in how different disciplines and approaches are brought together' (Szerszynski and Galarraga 2013, 2818, 2822). For Dena MacMynowski, clear differentiation is the key to good synthesis: 'in order for interdisciplinary research to proceed more transparently in terms of the recombination of ideas and making the power associated with knowledge claims explicit, interdisciplinary environmental research needs to consciously embark on a process of differentiation and clarification before, or while, moving toward synthesis' (MacMynowski 2007).

From many years thinking about and living in interdisciplinary spaces, we have learnt that this account of power confronted – in which differentials are acknowledged and addressed, and even occasionally overcome; or in which, at least, a model of interdisciplinarity less riven by relations of power is thought to be *imaginable* – is no less fantastical than the dream of mutuality with which we began. You can have all the frank conversations in the world with collaborators about the conditions

DOI: 10.107/9781137407962.0009

under which your exchanges are taking place; you can agree on a clear distribution of resources and labour throughout the collaboration; you can put in agreed strategies to ensure, as far as possible, that this will work; you can remain as open, and transparent, and clear, and dialogic as possible; but the reality is that financial and epistemic power is not distributed equally within the collaboration. That irrevocable state of affairs carries many *sequelae* in its trail. And everyone in the collaboration, in her heart of hearts, knows this.

After reciprocity

> What is it, then, that is desired in subjection? Is it a simple love of the shackles, or is there a more complex scenario at work? (Butler 1997, 27)

What would happen if we gave up on mutuality altogether? What if we abandoned the ideal of 'reciprocity'– not because it isn't realistic, but because it may not actually be desirable? Lately, and instead of adding our own analysis of how 'exchanges' might take place in interdisciplinary spaces, we have begun to wonder if new conceptualizations of interdisciplinarity would come into view if this term were not subject to the velvet stranglehold of mutuality. All of us who have collaborated, after all, have experience of doing so without any expectation either that everyone is on the same footing, or that meaningful forms of process, dialogue, and so on, will *actually* produce parity. So what if we just accepted, in the most basic sense, that if you're a humanities or social science person in an interdisciplinary neuroscientific project, then there is some likelihood that you're going to have to meet your interlocutors more than halfway, that the emotional labour of holding things together might well fall substantially to you, and that there's a good chance that you're going to have to take responsibility for much of the project 'housework'? What if, as a natural science person, you made peace with the fact that your collaborators will assume you have never thought through your field's problematic use of particular terms, that they will sometimes treat you as a kind of veil of rigour, granting them access to various pots of money, and then expect you, as one of the few scientists who can be bothered to attend 'interdisciplinary' meetings, to consistently represent all that is 'wrong' with your discipline?

DOI: 10.1057/9781137407962.0009

These are, we are quite aware, not the happiest of counsels. But the point we make in this chapter is three-fold. First, the advice consistently given to would-be collaborators – Make your goals clear! Know what your expertise is! Begin a frank dialogue! – bears no relationship to our and, we think, our collaborators' many experiences of working in inter-disciplinary projects, and of making space for our own interests within forms of financial, epistemic, and bureaucratic power that consistently produce those interests as contingent on the scientific questions in which they are entangled. Our natural scientist colleagues, similarly, will tell you many stories of their research interests being figured as inherently crude, reductive, and simplistic – of being imagined as dependent on the nuances of the cultural-historical questions that bear down upon *them*, in their turn. If you are going to live in such spaces, better to learn to live in them as they are, and give up on an agentic fantasy in which you will be able substantively to transform imbalances, inequalities, and existing norms governing epistemic (and other kinds of) potency.

Second, as two social scientists caught in this space, we have learnt neither to lament, nor to spend energy resisting, this state of affairs: what we have learnt, instead, is sometimes to subjugate (or at least accept the subjugation of) our work and our interests to the neuroscientific interests in which we seek to entangle them. To the extent that we, in order for our research interests to move forward, need 'the neuroscientists', and they can get on perfectly well without us (in our estimation, anyway), we remain intensely aware that we need to narrate our own research interests in ways that make sense to our collaborators, without much expectation that they will do likewise. If we often know more about cognitive neuro-science than any of our collaborators do about geography, sociology, the history of science, and so on – this is not because we find ourselves diligent, but because we find ourselves weak. (Again, we speak only from the social science perspective here; no doubt there is a mirror image of this point, from the point of view of neuroscientific collaborators, which we will not presume to ventriloquize.)

Third, what we are trying to emphasize here is that a *good enough* poli-tics of collaboration is not, in fact, exhausted by exhortations to frank speech and/or by demanding the recognition of one's epistemic and other contributions. One of the most important lessons we have learnt from our interdisciplinary work since 2008 (see especially Fitzgerald et al. 2014a) is that parity is overrated as a platform for exchange – that is, the fantasy of two more-or-less equal actors, exchanging their intellectual

DOI: 10.105/9781137407962.0009

goods in a spirit of reciprocal esteem, might not only be, in a basic sense, and like most fantasies, not 'true', but that it might also be more politically and epistemologically *inert* than has often been assumed. Because what this prim fantasy excises is any sense of risk and play – any sense of the intensity of a pleasure that might come from *giving one's self up to something and taking the consequences* (see e.g. Dean 2009). Indeed, the sociologist Andrew Balmer, in taking up this theme of subjugation, has analysed interdisciplinary relationships through the dynamics of playful sadomasochism, insisting, with Michel Foucault, that such scenes are not simple exercises in domination, but that they enact 'way[s] of creatively playing with strategic power to constitute new pleasures, new modes for engagement with each other and with the world more generally' (Balmer 2013). Balmer thus reminds us that there are intensely affective ethical and political structures, as well as forms of action and pleasure, located in such relational practices – practices that are, we would add, quite invisible to genteel exhortations to dialogue.

Interdisciplinarity and the reproduction of social power

We have cast ourselves, at least a few times, in this chapter as marginalized subordinates within spaces of great epistemological privilege. As we have stressed, we do not remain unaware of the ways in which 'we', and our disciplinary and epistemological preoccupations, are undoubtedly variously irritating to and undermining of the scientific and emotional labours of our collaborators; we are aware that, even if we too often feel ourselves to be under the scientific thumb, there are in fact many kinds of power – institutional, epistemic, managerial – that we can and do wield in interdisciplinary settings. But here is yet another objection to how we have positioned ourselves in this chapter – and another route through which we want to turn simplistic accounts of interdisciplinary power on their heads. We both have many colleagues, in our own disciplines (and in other disciplines from the humanities and the interpretive social sciences), who would gently point out that, from their perspective, our state of subjugation (such as it is) quite clearly has arisen from our having gotten ourselves into some very problematic spaces; that not only is it specious for us to cast ourselves as subjects of power, but that, in lending our support to, and expanding the reach of, scientific disciplines

DOI: 10.1057/9781137407962.009

(not least the neurosciences), *we throw our lot in with those disciplines* – that we are, in other words, co-producers of the very epistemic power from which we claim to distance ourselves (Cooter 2011, 2014). Worse (we caricature here): the sciences with which we are entangled have been the source of deleterious discourses on, for example, race, class, and gender; that scholars in the social sciences and humanities had long built up a conceptual armature to counteract such discourses; and that by mingling those concepts with the methods and theories of the neurosciences, people like us actually *evacuate* the space for such critical work. To the extent that people become raced, gendered, and classed subjects through particular relations of power, and to the extent that scientific research has bolstered and solidified such relations (*especially* when it is increasingly licensed to talk about social life) – then our dirge for subjugation starts to look hollow indeed.

This is a vexed and serious critique that we cannot do justice to here. It is undeniably true that neuroscientific research has been mobilized in deeply problematic ways (we say 'mobilized' to gesture at the frequent distance between research in the laboratory and its diverse applications). There is now an extensive body of research on the effects of neuroscientific discourses on policy, especially as that policy has been brought to bear on predominantly working-class and ethnic minority families (e.g. Edwards, Gillies and Horsley 2015; Lee, Macvarish and Lowe 2014; Pykett 2015). There is an even more prominent discourse about neuroscience and gender, which is often self-consciously essentializing (e.g. Baron-Cohen 2003) – resulting in popular claims that are, as the psychologist Cordelia Fine has pointed out, sometimes 'spurious' or 'misinterpreted' (Fine 2010, 283). 'The imaginative reader', Fine goes on,

> will not have too much difficulty envisaging how, by reinforcing stereotypes, such claims may affect people's social attitudes in ways that oppose progress toward greater gender equality, just as such claims did in the past. (Fine 2010, 283)

Against such invidious stereotypes, many will claim that the conceptual armature of the interpretive social sciences – culture, context, sociality, ideology, historical contingency, political decision-making, and so on – has helped to destabilize powerful scientific discourses, as they have been brought to bear (with or without the consent of their scientific progenitors) on many different kinds of people. This, many of our colleagues would remind us, is where the conversation about *power* in interdisciplinary neuroscience needs to be.

DOI: 10.1057/9781137407962.0009

And yet, at the heart of our different projects in this area, there has always been an intuition that a potent, (potentially) emancipatory politics of race, gender, class, or sexuality might not have to be always independent of the biological sciences. In pursing that intuition, we have been inspired, for example, by the work of the NeuroGenderings research collective, and by the potent forms of neurofeminism that many of the scholars within that loose agglomeration have insisted on locating at the heart of empirical brain research (Bluhm, Jacobson and Maibon 2012; Schmitz and Höppner 2014a, 2014b). We have learnt a great deal from scholars such as Gillian Einstein and Margrit Shildrick, who, in their reinvigoration of the politics of women's health, have always insisted on the complementarity of feminist theory and biological research on women's bodies (Einstein and Shildrick 2009). And we continue to be propelled by broader movements, within feminist theory, that are working to destabilize (to de-nature, we might say) the suturing of politics to critique, showing how feminist (and other social) theories might yet be traced through neurobiological histories and practices (Barad 2007; Rose and Abi-Rached 2013; Wilson 2004). If our own projects maintain a committed attention to the ways in which epistemic and cultural privileges can be put to work in the generation or sustenance of some deeply worrying relations of power, still, we have tried to show, in the empirical work that we have produced, that an interdisciplinary attention to brain and mind can also unsettle these relations in sometimes unexpected ways; that neuroimaging studies, themselves, can sometimes themselves be the bearers of critical practices.

Learning to live together

What are we to do, in the face of the unappetizing dynamics that have coursed through this chapter? One answer is: nothing. Donna Haraway, in her 'Companion Species Manifesto', surely the most compelling recent treatise on the complexity of relating through fraught boundaries, argues that 'all ethical relating is knit from the ... thread of on-going alertness to otherness-in-relation. We are not one, and being depends on getting on together' (2003, 50). Haraway's not-oneness, of course, is not a fantasy of always satisfied affiliation and exchange: humans' relationships with dogs are as filled with 'waste, cruelty, indifference, ignorance and loss', as much

DOI: 10.105/9781137407962.0009

as they are about 'joy, invention, labor, intelligence, and play' (2003, 12). Rather than simply seeking to resolve such a tension, Haraway, instead, makes an intellectual and ethical commitment to understanding, thinking, and working with and through the polyvalent realities of multispecies relation – a commitment that she names elsewhere as 'staying with the trouble' (Haraway 2010) – that is, of continuing to work on and in a world that, in all its inter-species relatedness, is quite inseparable from complex intertwinements of killing, and breeding, and companioning, and nurturing.

We and our collaborators are not quite different species, nor have we yet started killing each other. Still, in understanding the often uncomfortable dynamics of our own collaborative relating, we want to take Donna Haraway's injunction to heart. We want, in other words, as interdisciplinary scholars, not to seek mythical platforms for equal exchange, but to keep learning different ways of being unsettled together. In this sense, we want to abjure the fleeting comforts of frank-speaking, and the self-limiting, self-satisfying pleasure of confronting power; we want to say, in their place, that we are, in fact, willing to stay with the trouble of learning to live together.

Notes & Queries: 6

Q: *In terms of inequalities, asymmetries, and lack of parity, where would you say the particular pressure points frequently lie? What should I be mindful of, if and when I enter interdisciplinary spaces?*

A: While this is an important question, we should stress that we do not wish to paint interdisciplinary research as a kind of endlessly asymmetrical toiling – with the interdisciplinary researcher herself then only called upon either to manage, or live within, such unhappy relations of power. We *do* think that there is much more to be said about how power works in the interdisciplinary scene (certainly more than we have said here); more importantly, we want to suggest there is much to be gained from interdisciplinary collaborators at least becoming more alive to those dynamics, to how they work in their own right, but also to how they structure the emergence of the problem-space as such. To that end: there is a host of (usually) individually minor things that we (singly and together) have learnt to attend to, across a wide number of interdisciplinary

DOI: 10.1057/9781137407962.0009

collaborations – but which, systemized, and understood as an accumulation, may help to bring the power dynamics of a particular collaboration into understanding. We are not saying that these are inevitable – nor do they invariably position the social scientists and/or humanities people in the so-called 'weaker' position. And nor (though we have not at all paid enough attention to this dimension here) can they be abstracted from much thicker dynamics of race, class, and gender – which may not be visible on the surface of particular collaborations, but of course are significant determinants of the broader infrastructure from which those collaborations emerge (we need only think of the gendering of discipline at the university level, to see how such dynamics might become pertinent). An inexhaustive list of things to look out for would certainly include some of the following:

▶ Interdisciplinary research projects are made possible by a vital, and yet often undervalued and invisible, labour of 'housework' – ranging from paperwork, to dealing with university and research administrations, to ensuring that everyone in the collaboration is *okay*, and so on. Who does this work, and what value is assigned to it? How – at all – is it compensated? Who can get away with a small contribution to the housework, and who cannot?

▶ How – through which mechanisms, and drawing in which voices – is intellectual labour parcelled out in the project? Who is included in, or allowed to partake of, conceptual and 'philosophical' discussion – and who is expected to simply collect data?

▶ Who writes and structures an interdisciplinary grant? Who brings the team together? Who does the tedious labour of working out everyone's costs? Who is responsible (or makes themselves responsible) for getting it in on time?

▶ What kinds of adjudications are made about what is and isn't an important part of the project's process – and through which mechanisms are those adjudications made explicit or not? For example, is spending time reflecting on *how* one organizes a workshop as valued as the substantive labour of the workshop itself?

▶ Who does public engagement work – and how, and why? Sometimes public engagement can be seen as low status work; but sometimes, too, it can be a moment for the assertion of seniority. How is this kind of work positioned and distributed in a given

DOI: 10.1057/9781137407962.0009

collaboration? Which kinds of audiences are deemed worthy of cultivating? How – and where – does this cultivation take place?

▶ Thinking through appropriate 'outlets' for publication can reveal all sorts of dynamics. On the one hand, the logic of impact factors and h-indices often determine where (and by whom) labour is placed in writing; one the other, the general orientation of a journal may make implicit decisions about whose contribution is and is not going to be valued (e.g. how does neuroscientific work get positioned in a decision to submit an interdisciplinary paper to a cultural theory journal?). How – and by whom – do such decisions get made within a collaboration?

▶ Interdisciplinary, co-authored work of course (usually) needs to find some mid-range voice in which to articulate itself. But dynamics of power can sometimes structure both the relative claim that different disciplinary registers have *on* that middle range, as well as the pernicious maintenance of the fiction of a 'transparent language' (in other words, that one's one language represents the neutral position). How are registers of appropriate voice generated within the project? What do those voices sound like – and what legacies do they drawn upon?

▶ Sometimes expertise is considered fungible, and sometimes it is not; sometimes it is regarded as easily understandable, and some it isn't; some expertise is seen not as expertise but merely as 'common sense'. Focusing on such positioning and understandings of different expertise can often be a salutary experience in interdisciplinary work.

▶ When papers are co-authored, how and when do particular conventions from different disciplines get pulled in? Does the team follow the multi-authored conventions of the natural sciences (and the stratification of contribution that it implies), or does it follow the lone-muse humanities model (and the occlusion of *other* voices that thus becomes inescapable)? If artists are part of the collaborating team, has anyone worked to rethink practices of creative production (in relation to curatorship)?

DOI: 10.105/9781137407962.0009

OPEN

7

Feeling Fuzzy: The Emotional Life of Interdisciplinary Collaboration

Abstract: *Interdisciplinary collaboration is frequently considered hard intellectual and methodological labour. And it is that. But interdisciplinary work is emotional work too – and is riven by the presence of (and requirement to manage) many different kinds of feelings, not all of them joyful. This chapter takes up the analysis of emotion in interdisciplinary spaces – arguing that such spaces are deeply dependent on forms of emotional regulation. The chapter works through moments, from our own work, in which we have felt bad, confused, and irritated. Thinking through how we managed these moments, the chapter positions interdisciplinarity as an affectively fuzzy domain, and much of the work of collaboration as learning to live though that fuzz. The chapter is appended with an epilogue to the broader monograph, which focuses on the two authors' own form of collaborative labour.*

Keywords: affect; collaboration; emotion; emotional labour; emotional regulation; interdisciplinarity

Callard, Felicity and Des Fitzgerald. *Rethinking Interdisciplinarity across the Social Sciences and Neurosciences.* Basingstoke: Palgrave Macmillan, 2015. DOI: 10.1057/9781137407962.0010.

DOI: 10.105/9781137407962.00D

Quit your whining!

We are both participants in a carefully choreographed space that has been designed to elicit productive cross-disciplinary engagements between humanities scholars, life scientists, mind scientists, social scientists, artists, and engineers. The convenor uses the technique called 'open space', where a number of participants suggest topics for a discussion, and then each goes off somewhere and leads that discussion herself, with whomever else wants to participate.

Des suggests, to the larger group, the topic of 'emotional labour in interdisciplinary spaces': he wants to talk through some of the ways in which emotions (including disappointment, irritation, anxiety, upset, even the occasional bout of pleasure) press on, and thus shape, interdisciplinary spaces and research. There is a skipped beat – silence occupies the room for a short while, before several delegates (including the convenor, herself, who, by dint of her role qua *convenor, certainly knows about emotional labour) gather to join Des.*

One of our collaborators overhears someone nearby, from a discipline totally different from either of ours, say to her neighbour something along the lines of: "You go and have that session on emotions and emotional labour. But also, how about we quit whining and run a session on actually doing some work?"

This person was, of course, kidding. But her remark, like all the best put-downs, provoked us to think through something important: sure, it can be a relief to get your resentments and disappointments off your chest, but what do emotional labour, and reflections *on* that labour, have to do with 'actual work'? Why is it not simply *whining*? Leaving aside our suspicion that whining might, in fact, be an under-valued and understudied genre, this chapter is an attempt to answer that question. We argue, here, that not only is emotion work heavily implicated in research work, but the labour of interdisciplinarity is emotional in ways that depart from the regular affective challenges that accompany all collaborative endeavours. We are convinced that understanding interdisciplinarity in practice means understanding how, why, and with what consequences, interdisciplinary research spaces are underscored by thick, deep currents of often subsumed, and yet profoundly felt, emotion – whose sources and objects are often difficult to discern. And yet they can, when attended to, tell us a great deal about points of epistemological, ontological and political blockage within any interdisciplinary configuration. Those blockages, in turn, help us to understand which kinds of interdisciplinary crossings and exchanges are more or less possible or likely within that

DOI: 10.1057/9781137407962.0010

configuration – and hence why certain research questions, approaches and methodologies find fertile ground, while others sometimes run into the sand. In other words, emotional dynamics can have great power in enabling and closing down the pursuit of particular interdisciplinary research trajectories. To treat the emotional economy of interdisciplinary collaborative work as epiphenomenal to – rather than a significant shaper of – those cross-disciplinary research trajectories would be a mistake.

A second claim follows from such a diagnosis: collaborative work – *and especially interdisciplinary work of the kind that we discuss in this book* – is inseparable from particular forms of, methods for, strategies around, and investments in, *emotional regulation*. We have become convinced, in the course of the years that we have spent in these spaces, that when collaborators from very different disciplines work together, most of them depend significantly upon practices of emotional regulation. Such practices help to ensure that interdisciplinary collaborations do not fall apart, and are able – oftentimes – to result in collaboratively produced research. Notably, instances of emotional dysregulation can be startling indicators of moments at which regulatory practices have broken down; or of collaborators' deliberate calling of attention to the affectively freighted landscape in which they all are working; or of instances of interdisciplinary contestation that – for whatever reason – cannot be quickly subsumed back into the usual affective economy that characterizes any given interdisciplinary space. And when we think of this affective economy, we include not only researchers from all disciplines, but those such as project co-ordinators, convenors and facilitators. Their material and immaterial labour is indispensable in allowing interdisciplinary projects to get off the ground and to persist, though it is often invisible precisely because such labour threatens to be regarded as mere 'infrastructure'. (How gender – and gendered assumptions – work here is particularly important to attend to.) We want the chapter to illustrate how typical – and often banal – such feelings are. But we also want to use these affectively marked instances, and our analyses of them, to intervene in existing debates about what interdisciplinarity is like, and why it is often difficult to accomplish.

Affects and their regulation

There are two major theoretical preoccupations at the heart of this chapter. The first centres on why it is not enough to focus on *epistemological*

DOI: 10.1057/9781137407962.0001

differences between disciplines to understand the complications of inter-disciplinary spaces. On our account, it is often difficult to determine the origin, quality, and after-effects of interdisciplinary moments of pique, disorientation, and friction. Such states work, frequently, to confound any possibility of speaking out or acting clearly and decisively (i.e. acting in straightforwardly *agentic* or *political* ways) in response to them. When the source of an emotion is unclear (as it frequently is with feelings of irritation or slight malaise or embarrassment), what is produced is often a sense of affective confusion or bewilderment – one that is very distinct from emotions with a clear origin and a distinct object (such as fury against a particular individual or a particular theory she holds). Such bewilderment does not necessarily lessen through a process of *epistemo-logical* resolution. We are not simply describing, here, interdisciplinary situations in which a researcher feels confused because she does not have the knowledge base to understand the content of a collaborator's communication. Interdisciplinary spaces cannot be summed up, in other words, as spaces characterized by the movement from epistemo-logical confusion to reasoned – or at least momentary – clarity, in which researchers manage to overcome their initial epistemic differences and build shared knowledge together.

We linger over this point since it is so commonly the orienting framework used to understand interdisciplinary spaces. (Much of the existing literature on interdisciplinary teams, for example, focuses on how researchers *with different epistemic commitments* 'share and inte-grate their cognitive resources in order to produce new results that cut across disciplinary boundaries' (Andersen and Wagenknecht 2012, 1881).) Sianne Ngai, in her work on 'minor and generally unprestig-ious feelings', distinguishes feeling 'vaguely "unsettled" or "confused"', as an 'affective sense of bewilderment', from confusion that results from 'the epistemological sense of indeterminacy': such bewilder-ment – 'this feeling of confusion *about* what one is feeling' – might well, she suggests, be 'an affective state in its own right' (Ngai 2005, 14; italics in original). Our conjecture is that such kinds of 'affective disorientation' – to use Ngai's potent phrase – or of 'feeling fuzzy' (to use our own coinage) have been particularly common in the interdis-ciplinary spaces that we have inhabited. One of the purposes of this chapter is to begin to do justice to the important roles that these often ill-understood and often ignored affective states play in shaping the topologies and logics of interdisciplinary research.

DOI: 10.105/9781137407962.0010

We realize that complex emotions are central to many, if not all, forms of practice – whether research based or otherwise. Historians of science and of emotion have compellingly demonstrated how potent scientists' affective responses have been in the generation of scientific models, concepts and data – whether we are talking about scientists' reactions in the face of animals' emotions, Darwin's flinching, or early theories of artificial intelligence (Dror 2011; Smith 2014; Wilson 2009). There is a growing body of sociological literature on how emotions move and coalesce within research laboratories (Fitzgerald 2013; Kerr and Garforth 2015). But there is something distinct, we feel, about the contours of affect that have moved and passed through us in profoundly interdisciplinary (as opposed to more mono- or multi-disciplinary) spaces. Here, the methods that researchers use can be so heterogeneous; the discursive conventions that make certain elements of the scene unsayable or sayable are so often *not* shared across disciplinary differences; the epistemologies can be so various; researchers' modes of bodily comportment so distinct from one another; and the settling on a shared object of investigation is, at times, impossible. The orienting ethos of an openness to alterity (the alterity of others' methods, ontologies, and ways of 'doing' research) that tends to frame the normative horizons of interdisciplinary spaces (even if it often does not play out in practice) is also, we think, a terrain conducive to the emergence of the kinds of complex affective states (including bewilderment) that we are interested in here. Bodily, psychological, affective – as well as more straightforwardly 'epistemological' – fuzziness and friction are, we believe, not so prevalent in more straightforward mono-disciplinary spaces (where researchers often have some sense of shared modes of conversing and comporting themselves, even if they profoundly disagree with one another), or multi-disciplinary spaces (where there is more commonly a shared sense that no one is really *expected* to open herself to the other's methods or ontologies, and that each can return 'home' more or less unchanged by the encounter).

Second, there is value in recognizing the important role that the regulation – and dysregulation – of affective states plays as emotions pass between and through members of an interdisciplinary team, as well as through artefacts and technologies (email and other writing technologies can be particularly vexed sites) that are central to the workings of any interdisciplinary research project. By using the term 'regulation' we want to capture the various ways in which individuals' and groups' affective states might be modulated: we are interested in how mental processes,

DOI: 10.1057/9781137407962.0001

physiological processes, comportment, and gesture intertwine; we are *especially* interested in how the emergence of friction and fuzziness – as well as of more clearly contoured emotions – can easily produce, in turn, attempts to attenuate or sidestep such feelings and dispositions. This might be through consciously practised emotional 'regulation', or indeed, if those attempts fail, through states of individual and collective dysregulation. Dwelling at greater length on the routes that affective responses can and do take in interdisciplinary projects might thus provide some markers for the interdisciplinary researcher to find her way through such projects, while retaining (most of) her sanity.

This is not the first time that either of us has written on this topic. We have elsewhere published more formal pieces on the role of affect in the psychological and brain sciences, on feelings of awkwardness in one interdisciplinary project, on how 'affect' itself has often been the theoretical and empirical ground upon which scholars have sought to 'become interdisciplinary', and on the complex looping of blame (Callard et al. 2012b; Fitzgerald 2013; Fitzgerald et al. 2014a; Papoulias and Callard 2010). We draw on some of that work here. Additionally, and in line with our broader goals for this volume, we mine some of our own fairly mundane encounters in the interdisciplinary scene. We draw out small moments – of fuzziness and of other affective dispositions – from our own immersion in interdisciplinary projects and places, to show how we have come to see emotions as variously diagnostic of the situations in which we – and, indeed, some of our collaborators – have found ourselves.

Telling lies

In Chapter 2, we described the outline of an experiment on neuroscientific lie detection in which one of us (DF) was involved. Again, in brief, the basic intuition of this experiment was that if it is possible to intuit (from literary, historical, and sociological analysis) that untruth is not, in fact, a natural state that can be isolated to particular neurological functions, then what would happen if an experiment were conducted that induced participants to tell a particular kind of awkward *truth* in the brain scanner – a truth that would show brain activity broadly similar to that previously associated with the state of lying? Over three days, the collaborators tried to answer this question by recruiting a cohort of local choir singers, and formed them into two teams. They told the

DOI: 10.105/9781137407962.0010

participants that this was an experiment in team evaluation, and that they were to compete against one another in a series of tasks. Participants were told that events would culminate in a sing-off, in front of a famous local choir director – and they would then have individually to rate one another's performance, while in the brain scanner. Crucially, they were told the accuracy of these ratings would go into the overall evaluation. Unbeknownst to the participants, each team contained two actors, who were given two simple instructions: be very likeable, and sing *horribly*. When the participants came in to be scanned, after a long day's singing and competing, they thought they were evaluating other team members at random – but of course they all had to evaluate the nice-but-talentless actors. The research team hypothesized that telling the *truth* about those actors, in the scanner, would be really awkward, and socially potent, and cognitively taxing – exactly the cognitive functions, in other words, often associated with telling *lies*.

If this is a generic example of how a social-literary intuition (truth is a contextual phenomenon) might be threaded through a neuroscientific method to produce – potentially – a new insight, there was also a significant amount of emotional regulation involved in its execution. Throughout the procedure, there was a great deal of ambivalence and awkwardness: several of the experimenters involved retained an anxiety about whether this experiment was a good thing to be involved in; collaborators sometimes worried about what, precisely, they were contributing to the project and what, on the other hand, they were getting from it; people were occasionally irritated with one another (see Fitzgerald et al. 2014a from which this account partly draws). In one memorable early meeting where the project was presented to the wider laboratory hosting it, the lab members (as scientists will) got really stuck in to the specifics of the experiment, making several of the other experimenters worry about what this actually had to do with them anymore. And all of this is added, one can be sure, to the normal affective potency of doing an ecological experiment (the excitement of seeing actors move, unrumbled, through the participants; the tension of revealing the truth), as well as the kinds of bodily and emotional regulation necessitated by keeping up the pretence of the 'game' – and keeping the truth from the participants throughout.

But most significantly, perhaps, from DF's perspective, what was at stake throughout the experiment was a particular kind of *regulation* – which is to say, the collaborators tacitly practised a kind of internal

DOI: 10.1057/9781137407962.0001

management of their affective states *vis-à-vis* the project. DF would go so far as to say that the experiment worked out precisely *because* of the emotional regulation practised by the experimenters who were part of it. This was, on the one hand, an experiment that was pregnant with emotion (and in particular, with forms of awkwardness, taciturnity, sullenness, and so on). On the other hand, DF believes, from his own perspective, that the researchers, themselves, rarely addressed this with one another. While they kept up a lively critical dialogue, nonetheless, when researchers were frustrated with one another, they often kept it to themselves; when they thought the others were flat-out wrong, they sometimes swallowed it; when they felt as though they were being talked-down-to, they frequently let it go; most significantly, when they weren't sure whether this was a very good experiment, or whether it was especially something they wanted to be involved in, or whether it was ever going to work, and even if they cared either way, they of course thought and talked about it – but it also seemed to DF that they sometimes quelled these anxious, ambivalent feelings, or regulated them, and moved on.

This is what we intend to draw attention to when we talk about the importance of understanding and working with the manifold ways in which affects are modulated, inhibited, it and transformed in interdisciplinary research projects. When we invoke matters of affective regulation, we are not articulating a prim warning about the impropriety of emotional outbursts. Rather, we're pointing to how intensely affectively weighted interdisciplinary spaces often are, and, also, to the fact that attention to – and management of – that weight, might have a significant bearing on the success, or otherwise, of an interdisciplinary encounter.

Playa hater

> 'This room is filled with neuroscience playa haters.' Felicity overhears this comment made at a workshop that is assessing the current state of neuroscientific evidence and models. It features a very small number of neuroscientists, a large number of social scientists and humanities scholars; amongst them are several very outspoken critics of neuroscience.

The term 'playa hater' emerged in late 1990s rap to describe those who criticize the successful strivings of those (like rappers themselves) who

DOI: 10.105/9781137407962.0010

'made it' within a system not designed for them. (See, in particular, The Notorious B.I.G.'s 'Playa Hater', in which he sang about the two kinds of people in the world, today: the 'players' and the 'playa haters'.) What is going on here? First, in the move from 1990s rap to this researcher's diagnosing of the fractious – though, let's face it, rarefied – space of an interdisciplinary workshop on neuroscience? Second, in our deciding to include this culturally and historically dense moment, one that invokes a specific linguistic terrain, often associated with a particular kind of black masculinity, and that then uses that terrain to complexify what regular commentary might simply have characterized as predictable cross-disciplinary critique of neuroscience on the part of the humanities and social sciences?

First, let us consider the sentence, 'This room is filled with neuro-science playa haters.' FC believes this to be a moment of diagnosis, in which there was the identification (correct, FC believes) of some sense of grievance and envy on the part of at least some of those in the social sciences and humanities; as well as of a disparity in power between the neurosciences (strong) and those enviously attacking it (the weaker humanities and social sciences); as well as of the strangeness of running a conference about neuroscientific evidence that was filled with so many people 'outside' of the field and that contained so few practising neuroscientists. The sentence, on the one hand, can be interpreted as a powerful means both to gesture to a recent transformation in disci-plinary hierarchies (the neurosciences were thrust into the limelight at the same time as the humanities were feeling increasingly anxious about their status) and a means to install (not wholly ironically) anyone issuing the sentence close to the heart of interdisciplinary power. But there is more going on here, too. The term 'hater', as it has emerged in the last couple of decades, conveys a complex mesh of affects: the 'hater' not only is unable to be happy about the success of the person she or he is 'hating', but rather wants to undermine that person by attempting to expose her flaws or inadequacies. Here, then, is an acute analysis of the shape that critique of 'the neurosciences', on the part of humanities and social science scholars, can sometimes take. FC remembers the atmosphere in the workshop as, indeed, at times, hostile against 'neuroscience' – and hostile in a way that refused any real engagement with the heterogene-ous methods or epistemologies of the neurosciences, and that was force-fully committed to trying to identify as many flaws in 'neuroscience' as possible. She surmised that the use of the term 'hater', to describe some

DOI: 10.1057/9781137407962.0001

of those in the room, diagnosed the often disavowed affective underpinnings of a particular kind of critique that imagines itself as conducted on affectively neutral, reasoned, and deliberative grounds. The sentence, FC thinks, also expresses some bafflement that the neuroscientists in the room had been subject to such affectively intense critique, given that they were precisely those who had chosen to engage, in sustained ways, with those from other disciplines in order to interrogate neuroscientific models and evidence. But the affective dynamics of the workshop did not, FC believes, hold open the possibility of recognizing these kinds of 'entangled' cross-disciplinary labours: instead, they lurched towards a bifurcated field of 'haters' and 'playas'.

This overheard sentence, then, which might well usually have been sloughed off as a casual interjection and one unimportant to the 'work' of interdisciplinarity, made clear to FC how any attempt to understand that work needs to attend to the fraught and deep affective channels that shape how individual researchers – and the arguments they make – retreat, advance, exchange, and disengage with fields different from their own. The sentence achieved this through a bold and unexpected importation of popular culture – specifically via the use of a term that emerged in African-American hip hop to anatomize the changing economic and social hierarchies of the street and the music industry. We want to stress that, in our experience, it has not been uncommon for this kind of ironic, multi-modal word-play – an informal register that can carry irritation, acuity, grandiosity, and hurt more openly than that of frequently strangulated academic exchange – to be the means through which we ourselves, as well as others we have heard commenting on interdisciplinary scenes, bear witness to some of the most difficult elements of interdisciplinary working.

A quick postscript: The term 'playa hater' began to travel, sometimes invoked by us and by some of the people with whom we collaborate; it become a way to track interdisciplinary power dynamics. One of us (FC) has herself, on a number of occasions, been described, good-naturedly, as a 'neuroscience playa hater'. She certainly didn't easily identify with being one (not least given the unhappy analysis we have just provided above), and she certainly didn't see herself consciously wanting to endorse a bifurcated vision of the world in which there are simply the 'playas' and the 'playa haters'. She did, however, reluctantly have to acknowledge that she did recognize certain aspects of herself, as well as of the affectively fraught field of interdisciplinary research on the mind and brain, that

DOI: 10.1057/9781137407962.0010

the phrase 'playa hater' serves to conjure up. Let's face it, she'd felt the envy of the hater. In her potent analysis of 'ugly feelings', Sianne Ngai argues that 'envy lacks cultural recognition as a valid mode of publicly recognizing or responding to social disparities, even though it remains the *only* agonistic emotion defined as having a perceived inequality as its object' (Ngai 2005, 128). The temptation is always to tell the envious person to 'get over it' – where 'it' is a designator of the inadequacy of that individual's psyche – rather than to think through the imbrication of the psychological and the social so as to understand what it is that provokes the desire to inhabit (or to crush) the space of the other. It would be fair to say that FC hasn't 'got over it'; her envy is still strong. But the introduction – and then circulation – of the figure of the playa hater ended up, over time, having a significant effect on how she herself thought about, and indeed entered into, collaborations with those from other disciplines – as well as how she thought about the spatial logics of the interdisciplinary field in which she was a participant. The diagnostic precision of the phrase 'playa hater' perhaps allowed her, over time, to move from 'feeling fuzzy' about how such an appellation had ended up being attached to her, to being able to inhabit an interdisciplinary landscape that she was less likely to construe in such agonistic terms.

Coming from the outside

Here is another example, not only of the density of emotions in inter-disciplinary spaces, but of the ability of emotions both to unseat those experiencing them, as well as to orient the grooves down which inter-disciplinary research might go in the first place. This time, we focus on annoyance (see also Ngai 2005 on irritation). Some years ago, one of us (DF) applied for funding for a research project, in which he proposed – among other things – to interview people with a neurodevelopmental diagnosis about prospects for treatment (which were then remote, but certainly under investigation). His project, although grounded in the social sciences, was intended to work, in an interdisciplinary manner, through a larger bioscientific research endeavour – and to offer to that project, in exchange for its imprimatur, a sense of how service users and their families thought through issues around biomedical intervention. In the event, he wasn't funded, and the project never got off the ground – which is itself a banal and quotidian event. But what *was* interesting

DOI: 10.105/9781137407962.00D

was how the project proposal was reviewed – and, in particular, how at least one reviewer, through what DF read as a sense of frustration and irritation, positioned the proposal as a poorly-conceived, attempted intervention from the outside. 'I was deeply disappointed by this project for several reasons', the reviewer began: '... the candidate appears to believe that scientists are on the verge of developing a possible biological therapeutic intervention ... But this is simply not the case.' Indeed, DF's project in general 'display[ed] a shocking lack of familiarity with the state of biomedical science in this area.' Worse, the topic that he proposed to interview people about had 'no grounding in biomedical fact', while he had failed to 'familiarise himself with the literature' around the diagnosis in question. Indeed, his proposal 'illustrate[d] a degree of ignorance that is very disappointing', while his 'nonsensical framing' of his questions '("garbage in")' would only produce 'nonsensical data ("garbage out")'. 'Coming to a topic from the "outside" can sometimes be highly valuable', the review concluded, 'but the demands of a topic such as this necessitate some understanding of the nature of [this diagnosis] and how it affects people and their families ... '

There is a great deal that might be said here. The reviewer refers to DF as an 'outsider' to 'the field'. They position him as someone who is not simply wrong but in fact 'ignorant'. They locate his questions outside of the zone of respectable sense-making, position his failure as an absence of preparation, wonder if he has faced up to the 'demands' of the scientific material, and so on. But let us draw two things out in particular: first, the territorial dynamic of inside and outside, of expert and candidate, of serious research and garbage, within which these remarks are couched. We are not quibbling, here, over whether or not this project should have been funded: fine projects exhaust the limit of available research funds every day, and indeed we are quite willing to accept that the project in question did at least exhibit some of the deficiencies described. But what remains pertinent is the series of bifurcations in which the review was nonetheless couched – and, moreover, the proposal seems to have been read as a (poor) attempt to intervene in a bioscientific space, *from the outside*. Being adjudicated on such grounds – rightly or otherwise – is certainly one feature of trying to lead an interdisciplinary life. But we want to note, second, how *affectively* charged this exchange, conducted via the transfer of written materials, seems. We refer, here, not only to DF's own sense of annoyance, embarrassment, and so on, at these remarks, but to the intensity of *irritation* that DF reads in the review. Perhaps, indeed,

DOI: 10.1057/9781137407962.0010

he over-reads. But the language of disappointment, concern, and shock appears, at least initially to him, as otiose: the reviewer, after all, could have elaborated why he or she found the proposal deeply problematic without these affective supports. We want to raise the question, then, as this chapter progresses, of what we might conclude about the contemporary landscape of interdisciplinary research if we pay close attention to the affective structure in which this exchange is suspended.

Anti-political

At the end of the lie detection study discussed above, one of us (DF) and his colleagues wrote a more formal auto-ethnographic account of how it felt to participate in a social science/neuroscience collaboration. In coming to understand their project, the authors set themselves against a recent, high-profile account of collaboration (between natural scientists and social scientists) gone wrong, by Paul Rabinow and Gaymon Bennett (Rabinow and Bennett 2012). Whereas Rabinow and Bennett had argued for rather more frank speaking in highly-charged interdisciplinary spaces, DF and his colleagues suggested, in deliberate contrast, that:

> [our] success might have come precisely because we did not speak frankly; we did not seek the truth; we totally failed to acknowledge – let alone discuss – the consequences of our experimental situation. What we did, instead, was to try to work and live within a zone that was just about ambiguous enough to keep everything together – that was sufficiently averse to frank-speaking to keep the worst of the resentments at bay. (Fitzgerald 2014a, 716)

That paper became part of a wider set of interventions in which DF and FC, both separately and together, had been trying to think beyond the usual encomia for truth and frankness. We focused, for example, on what it meant to become a 'subject of collaboration' – and we suggested that such a becoming might mean learning to find joy and insight within some more ambiguous and confusing ethical structures than those espoused by frank speakers of collaborative truth (Fitzgerald and Callard 2014). This last contribution, hosted on an interdisciplinary blog, produced (indeed, to be fair, literally invited) a response from a group of scholars, led by Anthony Stavrianakis, and including Rabinow and Bennett – the tone of which seemed, to us at least, somewhat irate. The 'determined self-limitation' described in our work marked, for these

DOI: 10.1057/9781137407962.0001

authors, 'a troubling turn in the practice of truth and ethics' – suggesting a moment, indeed, in which researchers seemed willing to give up on:

> exercises of critical self-formation that prepare one to take up truth-practices in the face of shifting power relations and the attendant need to speak frankly about both power and the truth as one finds it. (Stavrianakis et al. 2014)

Worse, our espousal of the importance – and complexity – of play, over the need to seek clarity, was interpreted not as 'the uninhibited and spontaneous activity of scientific curiosity' (Stavrianakis et al. 2014), but, rather, as representing 'a species of ethically deformative bureaucratic administration' – one marked by (here the authors draw on Robert Merton and John Dewey) an ' "occupational psychosis" ' in which abilities become blind spots, and one begins to internalize 'the limitation of one's authority and competence'. Collaboration conducted under such conditions, Stavrianakis and his colleagues argued, is determinedly 'antipolitical – and not in the scientific sense of seeking objectivity, but rather in the self-delimiting sense of turning away from the demands of the day' (Stavrianakis et al. 2014).

We were dismayed, on reading this text, to find our investment in the multiplication of ethical repertoires in the present, and our attention to the possible insights of play, to be subject to a rebuke that seemed so committed to analyses of function and bureaucracy, of truth and ethics, of art and critique, as these had been elaborated in mid-century (masculine) social theory. Might it not have not occurred to us – within our self-reported confusion – that complex questions of ethics, justice, and practice were at stake? Worse, the 'agonistic friendliness' espoused by Stavrianakis and his colleagues, as a counterpoint to our enjoinment to play, seems only to reassert a rather obvious starting position, wrapped in a (surely) unsustainable model of collaborative subjectivity. In either event, it has nothing to say with regard to the object we are trying to understand, *viz.* the ethical and affective nuance of collaboration *in practice*. But what interests us more than these intellectual disagreements is the sense of – and here we are frank – patrician touchiness through which this rebuke took shape. When we talk about the need for emotional regulation in interdisciplinary spaces, we are referring to the requirement for the interdisciplinary researcher to habituate herself to such registers of critique – and not just stoically to withstand such a reproach, but to attempt to quell her own heartfelt desire to respond, in kind, in

DOI: 10.105/9781137407962.0010

her turn. The question that we have had, continually, to ask ourselves is: how are we going to make research happen, when the desire for (and our practice of) interdisciplinarity has introduced a state of such conceptual and normative suspension, that we find ourselves surrounded by colleagues who variously understand our work to be garbage, or see us as ethically deformed bureaucrats?

The feeling of what doesn't happen

This book disturbs the tendency, in writings about interdisciplinarity, to cleave to the terrain of ideas, disagreements, and knowledge claims – and, in so doing, to disavow the complex ripples, wrinkles, and patternings of affect that course through what is all-too-often assumed to be an unruffled plane of interdisciplinary interaction. We pay attention, here, to how those wrinkles get rubbed out, how they are sometimes smoothed over, and how, sometimes, they endure within and between the unsuspecting bodies of interdisciplinary researchers themselves. We have tried in this chapter to bring to visibility some of the political, methodological, ontological, and epistemological work that those emotions perform. We hope to have shown: (1) how emotion can be influential in carving out the perimeters of an interdisciplinary space (as well as determining who is inside and outside of it); (2) how researchers can engage in various tactics to ensure that collaboration does not entirely fall apart; (3) how political and ontological differences can be experienced affectively (and *vice versa*); (4) how the eruption of unexpected – and superficially unimportant – moments of affect can be diagnostic of important lines of conjunction and contestation within interdisciplinary spaces; and (5) how acknowledgement of affective bewilderment while in interdisciplinary spaces is easily misconstrued as either a deliberate or unwitting removal from the terrain of the political.

We worry that our inclusion of instances of mostly negatively valenced emotion has been done, at least in part, through some desire to seek sympathy, to settle scores, or to parade, in the interests of exhibitionism, shameful episodes of our own making. But we also want to insist that to decide not to attend to the movements and textures of, and manifold responses (whether regulatory or dysregulatory) to such emotion in interdisciplinary spaces, is to miss much of what is happening in them. If the would-be collaborator hears a strong note of caution – even

DOI: 10.105/9781137407962.00D

warning – in this chapter, she has not misinterpreted our intent. We really do want these incidents – minor and anecdotal as all of them are – to begin a conversation about the range, shape, and effects of such intersectional and affective moments within interdisciplinary spaces, and how those moments might be encountered.

We have drawn particular attention to emotional regulation not only to attend to modes of self-management that the interdisciplinary researcher is called to (although we take these very seriously). Focusing on 'regulation' has also been a way for us to think against the grain of mastery and frankness in the interdisciplinary scene; it has, in particular, helped us to move beyond the stentorian banalities of 'truth' and 'power' in writings on collaboration – and thereby to think about how interdisciplinary life might be lived through less conventional ethical and philosophical practices. Most importantly, turning to the metaphor (although it is not only a metaphor) of regulation has helped us to understand much better what is going in the empirical projects that have captured our (interdisciplinary) attention. There is, for example, no cut between the subject of our lie-detection experiment, wondering how or whether to tell awkward but necessary truths, and the experimenters themselves, constantly unsure about how they might (if they might at all) voice their own anxieties about the experiment. What we have called in this chapter 'feeling fuzzy', and the affectively precarious responses that the interdisciplinary researcher makes in the face of this destabilizing bodily and mental state – is not incidental to the kinds of precarious, awkward, ambiguous, anxiety-inducing topics with which she is precisely trying to get her hands dirty.

Notes & Queries: 7

Q: I worry about tensions and emotions in my interdisciplinary work – what advice do you have for dealing with these?

A: Our answer is going to sound like advice that is appropriate to any group of people working collaboratively together: how do temperament and discipline combine and diverge within and across individuals? How might one regard an eruption of affect – or the collection of affect around a particular person – as diagnostic of some of the things that are going on in and across the wider collaboration? Tracking a group's interdisciplinary processes, here, might

DOI: 10.1057/9781137407962.0010

be helpful – so as to bring to the surface how different and difficult these modes of working can be. There are bound to be rough spots in any such collaboration, and allowing all to acknowledge this might open up ways for things to move forward. It might also be helpful to acknowledge – across all members of the collaborative group – how psychologically, practically, and emotionally exhausting interdisciplinarity can be.

But perhaps it is worth staying *with* this feeling, rather than always labouring with the assumption that things need to be addressed or resolved (whether immediately or across the longer term). This is *not* to say that one cannot – or indeed, should not – speak up when experiencing this kind of exhaustion, or when otherwise pinioned by negative affect. Of course, sometimes relations are just uninterestingly bad, and people positioned in ways that are unacceptable: we do *not* advise, in such situations, simply to get over it, or to stay quiet. But what we *are* trying to say is: the affective weight of an interdisciplinary collaboration may be as much a datum to be considered as a situation to be managed. We have learnt so much about our own collaborations from such an attention – insight that would have been quite lost by insisting on, for example, clearing the air. The question then is: what might be learnt from the tensions and emotions that run through a particular project? What do they reveal about the broader intellectual and psychological structure in which the project is caught? What can they tell us about how interdisciplinary knowledge is produced? Might they ultimately help us – if, indeed, it is progress that we are after – to pin down the broader pressure points, and anxieties, and aches, that are ultimately *blocking* that progress?

DOI: 10.1057/9781137407962.0001

OPEN

Epilogue

Coming clean

We have been rather tight-lipped, it's fair to say, about the interdisciplinary collaboration whose contours we arguably have greatest access to – namely, the collaboration between the two of us. This book marks a distinct moment in a collaboration that is, as we write these words, five years old. We have, during those years, developed, contributed to, and found ourselves caught up in many kinds of experiments. They include experiments of thinking, writing (articles, chapters, now this book), applying (for grant funding), visiting (other laboratories), presenting (at conferences, at workshops), collecting data (of very different kinds), organizing (of workshops, of panels), and vacationing (after those conferences and workshops). And through those experiments has come, additionally, the experiment of friendship. The interdisciplinary has been, throughout, an object of shared enquiry, a descriptor of our own collaboration, and the butt of many of our jokes and frustrations.

When we met, in the rain, at the residential workshop with which we opened the book, we shared two things. First, we were (and are) both interpretive social scientists, and that cross-disciplinary descriptor felt increasingly salient as we slowly worked out that we were the only two in a room filled, largely, by psychologists, philosophers, and neuroscientists. Second, we both felt alienated by – if unable, at that point, fully to understand – the dominant logic of interdisciplinarity that was consolidating around

DOI: 10.1057/9781137407962.0011

us. So, we identified with one another both *vis-à-vis* our broad location within the academy, and *vis-à-vis* our shared unease with how we were being drawn into topologies that made us – though we knew not quite why, exactly – wary. It is tempting to imagine that the coming together of a geographer and sociologist is unremarkable as an interdisciplinary collaboration – not least given that each of us is an interpretive social scientist. But what has been one of the most surprising facets of our working with one another is coming to realize the enduring legacy of the overlapping, yet undoubtedly heterogeneous disciplinary histories, investments, and networks of citations that each of us brings to our conversations and our joint writing. The labour of understanding and working creatively with our differences from one another – in terms of epistemologies, politics, rhetorics, and the different texts, theoretical formulations, and arguments to which each of us tends to turn most readily – is arguably the foundation for much of the thinking that we have outlined here.

The words within this volume have been wiped clean of the profound moments of disorientation, of disagreement, of irritation, and of feeling fuzzy that each of us has experienced in attempting this joint work of theoretical, empirical, and pragmatic writing. We are aware of the trickiness (if not tricksiness) of a first-person plural narrative voice – by turns distancing, intimate, heavily deliberate, strangely unsettling. The 'we' leaves opaque the nature of the ties between those elements that make up the 'we'. The reader always already knows that 'they' can't really think and feel the same. Our narrative 'we', then, as it covers over the friction of the elements that make that 'we' up, comes to perform much of what we have alluded to previously – tongue-biting and compromise. There is, then, just as much to say about subjugation and incorporation in relation to our own practices of working together as there has been to say about those other collaborations we have discussed. But there is, as we have insisted throughout this volume, simultaneously the pleasure that comes from *giving one's self up to something and taking the consequences*. New things emerge in the world when one inhabits the other's arguments, when one is led down the paths of the other's preoccupations, and when one is absorbed by the other's milieu.

Every paragraph of this book has been written with the two of us sitting, side by side, on a long table, looking out at several of our collaborators who are sitting and standing and moving in front of us, in the large open-plan space that is the home of Hubbub. This strange geographical

DOI: 10.1057/9781137407962.001

intimacy – and the equally strange dynamics of exhibitionism and surveillance that characterized the scene that joins our dyad both to our collaborators and to members of staff employed by our funder (who have been able to watch the affectively fraught scene unfolding in front of them) – has made us more proficient and less anxious about finishing each other's sentences and subjecting each other's paragraphs to stringent revisions. If we have argued for a logic of experimental entanglement in our approach to the scene of interdisciplinary research surrounding the brain and mind, then such entanglement animates, too, our own experimental scene of thinking and writing. Entanglement complicates – it can act as a snare, or embarrassment, or hindrance. We have experienced all of these. But these complications and obstructions have not simply stymied us but opened new paths, new plots, new modes of being in relation – with one another, and with the other people, entities, and objects with whom our interdisciplinary enquiries are concerned.

DOI: 10.105/9781137407962.0011

References

Adelman, George. 2010. "The Neurosciences Research Program at MIT and the Beginning of the Modern Field of Neuroscience." *Journal of the History of the Neurosciences* 19 (1): 15–23.

Alaimo, Stacy, and Susan Hekman, eds. 2008. *Material Feminisms*. Bloomington, IN: Indiana University Press.

Alberts, Bruce, Alexander Johnson, Julian Lewis, Martin Raff, Keith Roberts, and Peter Walter. 2002. *Molecular Biology of the Cell. 4 edition. The Extracellular Matrix of Animals*. New York, NY: Garland Science. Available from http://www.ncbi.nlm.nih.gov/books/NBK26810/. Accessed 3 September 2015.

Ali, Sabrina S., Michael Lifshitz, and Amir Raz. 2014. "Empirical Neuroenchantment: From Reading Minds to Thinking Critically." *Frontiers in Human Neuroscience* 8: 357.

Amodio, David M., and Chris D. Frith. 2006. "Meeting of Minds: The Medial Frontal Cortex and Social Cognition." *Nature Reviews Neuroscience* 7 (4): 268–277.

Andersen, Hanne, and Susann Wagenknecht. 2012. "Epistemic Dependence in Interdisciplinary Groups." *Synthese* 190 (11): 1881–1898.

Ankeny, Rachel A., Sabina Leonelli, Nicole C. Nelson, and Edmund Ramsden. 2014. "Making Organisms Model Human Behavior: Situated Models in North-American Alcohol Research, since 1950." *Science in Context* 27 (3): 485–509.

Arts & Humanities Research Council. 2015. "Science in Culture: Theme Overview." *Arts and Humanities Research Council*. http://www.ahrc.ac.uk/Funding-

DOI: 10.1057/9781137407962.0021

Opportunities/Research-funding/Themes/Science-in-Culture/Pages/
Science-in-Culture.aspx. Accessed 3 September 2015.

Association of Neuroesthetics. 2015. "Association of Neuroesthetics."
http://www.association-of-neuroesthetics.org. Accessed 15 July 2015.

Atkinson, Sarah, Bethan Evans, Angela Woods, and Robin Kearns.
2015. "'The Medical' and 'Health' in a Critical Medical Humanities."
Journal of Medical Humanities 36 (1): 71–81 .

Balmer, Andrew S. 2013. "Play in Interdisciplinary Collaboration
between Natural and Social Scientists." Presented at the STS
Seminar Series, University College London. https://www.academia.
edu/3616694/Play_in_Interdisciplinary_Collaboration_between_
Natural_and_Social_Scientists. Accessed 3 September 2015.

Balmer, Andrew S., Kate J. Bulpin, Jane Calvert, Matthew Kearnes,
Adrian Mackenzie, Claire Marris, Paul Martin, Susan Molyneux-
Hodgson, and Pablo Schyfter. 2012. "Towards a Manifesto for
Experimental Collaborations between Social and Natural Scientists."
https://experimentalcollaborations.wordpress.com/2012/07/03/
towards-a-manifesto-for-experimental-collaborations-between-
social-and-natural-scientists/. Accessed 3 September 2015.

Barad, Karen. 2007. *Meeting the Universe Halfway: Quantum Physics
and the Entanglement of Matter and Meaning.* Durham, NC: Duke
University Press.

———. 2008. "Posthumanist Performativity: Toward an Understanding
of How Matter Comes to Matter." In *Material Feminisms*, edited by
Stacy Alaimo and Susan Hekman, 120–156. Bloomington, IN: Indiana
University Press.

———. 2011. "Erasers and Erasures: Pinch's Unfortunate 'Uncertainty
Principle.'" *Social Studies of Science* 41 (3): 443–454.

Baron-Cohen, Simon. 2003. *The Essential Difference: The Truth about the
Male and Female Brain.* New York: Basic Books.

Barry, Andrew, and Georgina Born. 2013. "Interdisciplinarity:
Reconfigurations of the Social and Natural Sciences." In
Interdisciplinarity: Reconfigurations of the Social and Natural Sciences,
edited by Andrew Barry and Georgina Born, 1–56. London: Routledge.

Barry, Andrew, Georgina Born, and Gisa Weszkalnys. 2008. "Logics of
Interdisciplinarity." *Economy and Society* 37 (1): 20–49.

Bartlett, Christopher A., and Sumantra Ghoshal. 1990. "Matrix
Management: Not a Structure, a Frame of Mind." *Harvard Business
Review* 68 (4): 138–145.

DOI: 10.1057/9781137407962.0012

Bennett, Craig M., George L. Wolford, and Michael B. Miller. 2009. "The Principled Control of False Positives in Neuroimaging." *Social Cognitive and Affective Neuroscience* 4 (4): 417–422.

Berlant, Lauren, and Lee Edelman. 2014. *Sex, or the Unbearable*. Durham, NC: Duke University Press.

Berson, Josh. 2015. *Computable Bodies: Instrumented Life and the Human Somatic Niche*. London: Bloomsbury Academic.

BIOS. 2015. "About Us." *BIOS*. http://www.bios-research.com/. Accessed 24 July 2015.

Biswal, Bharat, F. Zerrin Yetkin, Victor M. Haughton, and James S. Hyde. 1995. "Functional Connectivity in the Motor Cortex of Resting Human Brain Using Echo-Planar MRI." *Magnetic Resonance in Medicine* 34 (4): 537–541.

Blackman, Lisa. 2014. "Affect and Automaticy: Towards an Analytics of Experimentation." *Subjectivity* 7 (4): 362–384.

Bluhm, Robyn, Anne Jaap Jacobson, and Heidi Lene Maibon, eds. 2012. *Neurofeminism: Issues at the Intersection of Feminist Theory and Cognitive Science*. London: Palgrave Macmillan.

Braidotti, Rosi. 2010. "The Politics of 'Life Itself' and New Ways of Dying." In *New Materialisms: Ontology, Agency, and Politics*, edited by Diana H. Coole and Frost Frost, 201–220. Durham, NC: Duke University Press.

Butler, Judith. 1993. *Bodies That Matter: On the Discursive Limits of "Sex."* New York: Routledge.

———. 1997. *The Psychic Life of Power: Theories in Subjection*. Stanford, CA: Stanford University Press.

Byrne, Sarah. 2014. "Interdisciplinary Research: Why It's Seen as a Risky Route." *The Guardian*, February 19. http://www.theguardian.com/higher-education-network/blog/2014/feb/19/interdisciplinary-research-universities-academic-careers. Accessed 3 September 2015.

Cacioppo, John T. 2002. *Foundations in Social Neuroscience*. Boston, MA: MIT Press.

Cacioppo, John T., and Gary G. Berntson. 1992. "Social Psychological Contributions to the Decade of the Brain: Doctrine of Multilevel Analysis." *American Psychologist* 47 (8): 1019–1028.

Cacioppo, John T., Stephanie Cacioppo, Stephanie Dulawa, and Abraham A. Palmer. 2014. "Social Neuroscience and Its Potential Contribution to Psychiatry." *World Psychiatry* 13 (2): 131–139.

DOI: 10.1057/9781137407962.0021

Callard, Felicity. 2003. "The Taming of Psychoanalysis in Geography." *Social & Cultural Geography* 4 (3): 295–312.

———. 2013. "Consulting Rooms: Notes towards a Historical Geography of the Psychoanalytic Setting." In *Psychoanalytic Geographies*, edited by Paul Kingsbury and Steve Pile, 73–78 Farnham, Surrey: Ashgate.

Callard, Felicity, and Des Fitzgerald. 2014. "Experimental Control: What Does It Mean for a Participant to 'Feel Free'?" *Consciousness and Cognition* 27 (July): 231–232.

Callard, Felicity, Des Fitzgerald, and Angela Woods. 2015. "Interdisciplinary Collaboration in Action: Tracking the Signal, Tracing the Noise." *Palgrave Communications* 1 (July): 15019.

Callard, Felicity, Des Fitzgerald, Simone Kühn, and Ulla Schmid. 2012a. "Experimental Entanglements in Cognitive Neuroscience." https://experimentalentanglements.wordpress.com. Accessed 3 September 2015.

Callard, Felicity, and Daniel S. Margulies. 2011. "The Subject at Rest: Novel Conceptualizations of Self and Brain from Cognitive Neuroscience's Study of the 'resting State.'" *Subjectivity* 4 (3): 227–257.

———. 2014. "What We Talk about When We Talk about the Default Mode Network." *Frontiers in Human Neuroscience* 8: 619.

Callard, Felicity, Jonathan Smallwood, and Daniel S. Margulies. 2012. "Default Positions: How Neuroscience's Historical Legacy Has Hampered Investigation of the Resting Mind." *Frontiers in Cognition* 3: 321.

Callard, Felicity, Diana Rose, and Til Wykes. 2012. "Close to the Bench as well as at the Bedside: Involving Service Users in All Phases of Translational Research." *Health Expectations* 15 (4): 389–400.

Callard, Felicity, Diana Rose, Emma-Louise Hanif, Jody Quigley, Kathryn Greenwood, and Til Wykes. 2012b. "Holding Blame at Bay? 'Gene Talk' in Family Members' Accounts of Schizophrenia Aetiology." *BioSocieties* 7 (3): 273–293.

Callard, Felicity, Jonathan Smallwood, Johannes Golchert, and Daniel S. Margulies. 2013. "The Era of the Wandering Mind? Twenty-First Century Research on Self-Generated Mental Activity." *Frontiers in Perception Science* 4: 891.

Cantor, David, and Edmund Ramsden, eds. 2014. *Stress, Shock, and Adaptation in the Twentieth Century*. Rochester, NY: University of Rochester Press.

Center for Neuroscience & Society, University of Pennsylvania. 2015. "Neuroscience Boot Camp." http://neuroethics.upenn.edu/neuroscience-boot-camp. Accessed 3 September 2015.

DOI: 10.105/9781137407962.0012

Chiao, Joan Y. 2009. "Cultural Neuroscience: A Once and Future Discipline." *Progress in Brain Research* 178: 287–304.

Choudhury, Suparna, Saskia Kathi Nagel, and Jan Slaby. 2009. "Critical Neuroscience: Linking Neuroscience and Society through Critical Practice." *BioSocieties* 4: 61–77.

Choudhury, Suparna. 2010. "Culturing the Adolescent Brain: What Can Neuroscience Learn from Anthropology?" *Social Cognitive and Affective Neuroscience* 5 (2–3): 159–167.

Choudhury, Suparna, and Jan Slaby, eds. 2012. *Critical Neuroscience: A Handbook of the Social and Cultural Contexts of Neuroscience.* Chichester, W. Sussex: Wiley-Blackwell.

Choudhury, Suparna, Jan Slaby, and Daniel S. Margulies. 2015. "Research Topic: Critical Neuroscience: The Context and Implications of Human Brain Research." *Frontiers.* http://journal. frontiersin.org/researchtopic/1708/critical-neuroscience-the-context-and-implications-of-human-brain-research. Accessed 30 July 2015.

Collier, Stephen J. n.d. "The Collaboratory Form in Contemporary Anthropology." The Anthropology of the Contemporary Research Collaboratory (www.anthropos-lab.net). http://anthropos-lab.net/ wp/publications/2007/01/the-collaboratory-form-in-contemporary-anthropology.pdf. Accessed 3 September 2015.

Cooter, Roger. 2011. "Re-Presenting the Future of Medicine's Past: Towards a Politics of Survival." *Medical History* 55 (3): 289–294.

———. 2014. "Neural Veils and the Will to Historical Critique: Why Historians of Science Need to Take the Neuro-Turn Seriously." *Isis* 105 (1): 145–154.

Costandi, Mo. 2008. "EMBL NeuroSchool." *Neurophilosophy.* http:// scienceblogs.com/neurophilosophy/2008/04/03/embl-neuroschool. Accessed 3 September 2015.

Critical Neuroscience. n.d. "Critical Neuroscience." http://www.critical-neuroscience.org. Accessed 3 September 2015.

Cromby, John, Tim Newton, and Simon J. Williams. 2011. "Neuroscience and Subjectivity." *Subjectivity* 4 (3): 215–226.

Davies, Gail. 2010. "Captivating Behaviour: Mouse Models, Experimental Genetics and Reductionist Returns in the Neurosciences." *The Sociological Review* 58 (May): 53–72.

Dean, Tim. 2009. *Unlimited Intimacy: Reflections on the Subculture of Barebacking.* Chicago, IL: University of Chicago Press.

DOI: 10.1057/9781137407962.0012

Despret, Vinciane. 2004. "The Body We Care for: Figures of Anthropo-Zoo-Genesis." *Body & Society* 10 (2–3): 111–134.

Dimock, Wai Chee. 2001. "Deep Time: American Literature and World History." *American Literary History* 13 (4): 755–775.

———. 2008. *Through Other Continents: American Literature across Deep Time*. Princeton, NJ: Princeton University Press.

Dror, Otniel. 2011. "Seeing the Blush: Feeling Emotions." In *Histories of Scientific Observation*, edited by Lorraine Daston and Elizabeth Lunbeck, 326–348. Chicago, IL.: University of Chicago Press.

Dumit, Joseph. 2004. *Picturing Personhood: Brain Scans and Biomedical Identity*. Princeton, NJ: Princeton University Press.

Durham University. n.d. "2014 Interdisciplinary Conference. Transfusion and Transformation: The Creative Potential of Interdisciplinary Knowledge Exchange." https://www.dur.ac.uk/ias/2014conference. Accessed 29 September 2015.

Dussauge, Isabelle, and Anelis Kaiser. 2012. "Neuroscience and Sex/Gender." *Neuroethics* 5 (3): 211–215.

Dzeng, Elizabeth. 2013. "How to Inspire Interdisciplinarity: Lessons from the Collegiate System." *The Guardian*. March 15. http://www.theguardian.com/higher-education-network/blog/2013/mar/15/interdisciplinary-academic-universities-research. Accessed 3 September 2015.

Economic and Social Research Council. 2013. "Transforming Social Science." http://www.esrc.ac.uk/news-and-events/press-releases/26437/transforming-social-science.aspx. Accessed 3 September 2015.

Edelman, Lee. 2004. *No Future: Queer Theory and the Death Drive*. Durham, NC: Duke University Press.

Edwards, Rosalind, Val Gillies, and Nicola Horsley. 2015. "Early Intervention and Evidence-Based Policy and Practice: Framing and Taming." *Social Policy and Society* Online First. doi:10.1017/S1474746415000081.

Einstein, Gillian, and Margrit Shildrick. 2009. "The Postconventional Body: Retheorising Women's Health." *Social Science & Medicine* 69 (2): 293–300.

Engerman, David C. 2015. "The Pedagogical Purposes of Interdisciplinary Social Science: A View from Area Studies in the United States." *Journal of the History of the Behavioral Sciences* 51 (1): 78–92.

European Commission. n.d. "Social Sciences & Humanities." *Horizon 2020: The EU Framework Programme for Research and Innovation*. http://ec.europa.eu/programmes/horizon2020/en/area/social-sciences-humanities#Article. Accessed 3 September 2015.

DOI: 10.1057/9781137407962.0012

European Network of National Networks studying Gene-Environment Interactions in Schizophrenia (EU–GEI), Jim van Os, Bart P. Rutten, Inez Myin-Germeys, Philippe Delespaul, Wolfgang Viechtbauer, Catherine van Zelst, et al. 2014. "Identifying Gene-Environment Interactions in Schizophrenia: Contemporary Challenges for Integrated, Large-Scale Investigations." *Schizophrenia Bulletin* 40 (4): 729–736.

European Neuroscience and Society Network. n.d. "European Neuroscience and Society Network." http://www.kcl.ac.uk/sspp/departments/sshm/research/ENSN/European-Neuroscience-and-Society-Network.aspx. Accessed 3 September 2015.

Faris, Robert E. L., and H. Warren Dunham. 1939. *Mental Disorders in Urban Areas: An Ecological Study of Schizophrenia and Other Psychoses.* Chicago, IL: Chicago University Press.

Farrer, C., and C. D. Frith. 2002. "Experiencing Oneself vs Another Person as Being the Cause of an Action: The Neural Correlates of the Experience of Agency." *NeuroImage* 15 (3): 596–603.

Fernyhough, Charles, Angela Woods, and Victoria Patton, eds. 2015. *Working Knowledge: Transferable Methodology for Interdisciplinary Research.* http://www.workingknowledgeps.com. Accessed 3 September 2015.

Ferraro, Kenneth F., and Tetyana Pylypiv Shippee. 2009. "Aging and Cumulative Inequality: How Does Inequality Get Under the Skin?" *The Gerontologist* 49 (3): 333–343.

Filevich, Elisa, Patricia Vanneste, Marcel Brass, Wim Fias, Patrick Haggard, and Simone Kühn. 2013. "Brain Correlates of Subjective Freedom of Choice." *Consciousness and Cognition* 22 (4): 1271–1284.

Fine, Cordelia. 2010. *Delusions of Gender: How Our Minds, Society, and Neurosexism Create Difference.* New York, NY: W. W. Norton.

Fitzgerald, Des. 2013. "The Affective Labour of Autism Neuroscience: Entangling Emotions, Thoughts and Feelings in a Scientific Research Practice." *Subjectivity* 6 (2): 131–152.

Fitzgerald, Des, and Felicity Callard. forthcoming. "Entangling the Medical Humanities." In *Edinburgh Companion to the Critical Medical Humanities*, edited by Anne Whitehead, Angela Woods, Sarah Atkinson, Jane Macnaughton, and Jennifer Richards. Edinburgh: Edinburgh University Press.

———. 2015. "Social Science and Neuroscience beyond Interdisciplinarity: Experimental Entanglements." *Theory, Culture & Society* 32 (1): 3–32.

———. 2014. "Entangled in the Collaborative Turn: Observations from the Field." http://somatosphere.net/2014/11/entangled.html. Accessed 3 September 2015.

DOI: 10.1057/9781137407962.0021

Fitzgerald, Des, Nikolas Rose, and Ilina Singh. forthcoming. "Revitalising Sociology: Urban Life and Mental Illness between History and the Present." *British Journal of Sociology*.

Fitzgerald, Des, Melissa M. Littlefield, Kasper J. Knudsen, James Tonks, and Martin J. Dietz. 2014a. "Ambivalence, Equivocation and the Politics of Experimental Knowledge: A Transdisciplinary Neuroscience Encounter." *Social Studies of Science* 44 (5): 701–721.

Fitzgerald, Des, Svenja Matusall, Joshua Skewes, and Andreas Roepstorff. 2014b. "What's so Critical about Critical Neuroscience? Rethinking Experiment, Enacting Critique." *Frontiers in Human Neuroscience* 8: 365.

Fondation Brocher. n.d. "Overview of the Brocher Foundation." www. brocher.ch. http://www.brocher.ch/en/brocher-fundation-in-brief. Accessed 3 September 2015.

Fontaine, Philippe. 2015. "Introduction: The Social Sciences in a Cross-Disciplinary Age." *Journal of the History of the Behavioral Sciences* 51 (1): 1–9.

Fotopoulou, Aikaterini, Donald W. Pfaff, and Martin A. Conway, eds. 2012. *From the Couch to the Lab: Trends in Psychodynamic Neuroscience.* Oxford: Oxford University Press.

Foucault, Michel. 1982. "The Subject and Power." *Critical Inquiry* 8 (4): 777–795.

Frazzetto, Giovanni. 2011. "Teaching How to Bridge Neuroscience, Society, and Culture." *PLoS Biology* 9 (10): e1001178.

Freed, Peter. 2008. "Research Digest." *Neuropsychoanalysis* 10 (1): 101–104.

Friedli, Lynne, and Robert Stearn. 2015. "Positive Affect as Coercive Strategy: Conditionality, Activation and the Role of Psychology in UK Government Workfare Programmes." *BMJ Medical Humanities* 41: 40–47.

Galea, Sandro. 2011. "The Urban Brain: New Directions in Research Exploring the Relation between Cities and Mood–anxiety Disorders." *Depression and Anxiety* 28 (10): 857–862.

Gallagher, Sean. 2000. "Philosophical Conceptions of the Self: Implications for Cognitive Science." *Trends in Cognitive Sciences* 4 (1): 14–21.

Ganzel, Barbara L., Pamela A. Morris, and Elaine Wethington. 2010. "Allostasis and the Human Brain: Integrating Models of Stress from the Social and Life Sciences." *Psychological Review* 117 (1): 134–174.

Gardner, Susan K. 2012. "Paradigmatic Differences, Power, and Status: A Qualitative Investigation of Faculty in One Interdisciplinary

DOI: 10.1057/9781137407962.0012

Research Collaboration on Sustainability Science." *Sustainability Science* 8 (2): 241–252.

Geertz, Clifford. 1973. *The Interpretation of Cultures*. New York: Basic Books.

Goldman, Alvin I. 2006. *Simulating Minds: The Philosophy, Psychology, and Neuroscience of Mindreading*. Oxford: Oxford University Press.

Goldstein, Kurt. 1995 [1934]. *The Organism: A Holistic Approach to Biology Derived from Pathological Data in Man*. New York: Zone Books.

Graff, Harvey J. 2015. *Undisciplining Knowledge: Interdisciplinarity in the Twentieth Century*. Baltimore, MD: Johns Hopkins University Press.

Greco, Monica. 2005. "On the Vitality of Vitalism." *Theory, Culture & Society* 22 (1): 15–27.

———. 2013. "Logics of Interdisciplinarity: The Case of Medical Humanities." In *Interdisciplinarity: Reconfigurations of the Social and Natural Sciences*, edited by Andrew Barry and Georgina Born, 226–246. London and New York: Routledge.

Greenwood, Kathryn, Chi-Fa Hung, Maria Tropeano, Peter McGuffin, and Til Wykes. 2011. "No Association between the Catechol-O-Methyltransferase (COMT) val158met Polymorphism and Cognitive Improvement Following Cognitive Remediation Therapy (CRT) in Schizophrenia." *Neuroscience Letters* 496 (2): 65–69.

Grosz, Elizabeth A. 2004. *The Nick of Time: Politics, Evolution, and the Untimely*. Durham, NC: Duke University Press.

Gupta, Akhil, and James Ferguson. 1992. "Beyond 'Culture': Space, Identity, and the Politics of Difference." *Cultural Anthropology* 7 (1): 6–23.

Gusnard, Deborah A., and Marcus E. Raichle. 2001. "Searching for a Baseline: Functional Imaging and the Resting Human Brain." *Nature Reviews Neuroscience* 2 (10): 685–694.

Hagouel, Anthony. 2012. "Duke Program Blends Neuroscience and Humanities." *The Duke Chronicle*, November 9. http://www.dukechronicle.com/article/duke-program-blends-neuroscience-and-humanities. Accessed 3 September 2015.

Haraway, Donna. 1985. "Manifesto for Cyborgs: Science, Technology, and Socialist Feminism in the 1980s." *Socialist Review* 89: 65–108.

———. 1997. *Modest_Witness@Second_Millennium.FemaleMan_Meets_OncoMouse: Feminism and Technoscience*. London: Routledge.

———. 2003. *The Companion Species Manifesto*. Chicago: Prickly Paradigm Press.

DOI: 10.1057/9781137407962.002

———. 2010. "Staying with the Trouble: Xenoecologies of Home for Companions in the Contested Zones." *Fieldsights – From the Editorial Office, Cultural Anthropology Online.* July 27. http://www.culanth.org/fieldsights/289-staying-with-the-trouble-xenoecologies-of-home-for-companions-in-the-contested-zones.

Harrison, Paul. 2007. " 'How Shall I Say It … ?' Relating the Nonrelational." *Environment and Planning A* 39 (3): 590–608.

Haueis, Philipp. 2014. "Meeting the Brain on Its Own Terms." *Frontiers in Human Neuroscience* 8: 815.

Heinz, Andreas, Daniel J. Müller, Sören Krach, Maurice Cabanis, and Ulrike P. Kluge. 2014. "The Uncanny Return of the Race Concept." *Frontiers in Human Neuroscience* 8: 836.

Hertzman, Clyde, and Tom Boyce. 2010. "How Experience Gets under the Skin to Create Gradients in Developmental Health." *Annual Review of Public Health* 31: 329–347.

Holmes, Emily A., Michelle G. Craske, and Ann M. Graybiel. 2014. "Psychological Treatments: A Call for Mental-Health Science." *Nature* 511 (7509): 287–289.

Horwitz, Ralph I., Mark R. Cullen, Jill Abell, and Jennifer B. Christian. 2013. "(De)Personalized Medicine." *Science* 339 (6124): 1155–1156.

Hubbub. 2015. "Transforming How We Understand Rest." http://hubbubgroup.org. Accessed 18 May 2013.

Hurlburt, Russell T., and Sarah A. Akhter. 2006. "The Descriptive Experience Sampling Method." *Phenomenology and the Cognitive Sciences* 5 (3–4): 271–301.

Hyman, Steven E. 2009. "How Adversity Gets under the Skin." *Nature Neuroscience* 12 (3): 241–243.

Interacting Minds Centre. 2015. "About the Centre." http://interactingminds.au.dk/about-the-centre. Accessed 3 September 2015.

Jack, Anthony Ian, and Andreas Roepstorff. 2002. "Introspection and Cognitive Brain Mapping: From Stimulus–response to Script–report." *Trends in Cognitive Sciences* 6 (8): 333–339.

Jackson, Mark. 2013. *The Age of Stress: Science and the Search for Stability.* Oxford: Oxford University Press.

Joel, Daphna, Ricardo Tarrasch, Zohar Berman, Maya Mukamel, and Effi Ziv. 2014. "Queering Gender: Studying Gender Identity in 'Normative' Individuals." *Psychology & Sexuality* 5 (4): 291–321.

DOI: 10.1057/9781137407962.0012

Jones, Owen D., Anthony D. Wagner, David L. Faigman, and Marcus E. Raichle. 2013. "Neuroscientists in Court." *Nature Reviews Neuroscience* 14 (10): 730–736.

Kafka, Ben. 2012. *The Demon of Writing: Powers and Failures of Paperwork.* New York: Zone Books.

Kaiser, Anelis, Sven Haller, Sigrid Schmitz, and Cordula Nitsch. 2009. "On Sex/gender Related Similarities and Differences in fMRI Language Research." *Brain Research Reviews* 61 (2): 49–59.

Kerr, Anne, and Lisa Garforth. 2015. "Affective Practices, Care and Bioscience: A Study of Two Laboratories." *The Sociological Review.* doi:10.1111/1467-954X.12310.

Klitz, William. 2014. "Whitey Crumbles." *Trends in Genetics* 30 (12): 516–518.

Knorr Cetina, Karin. 1992. "The Couch, the Cathedral, and the Laboratory: On the Relationship between Experiment and Laboratory in Science." In *Science as Practice and Culture*, edited by Andrew Pickering, 113–138. Chicago, IL: University of Chicago Press.

Krabbendam, Lydia, Christine I. Hooker, and André Aleman. 2014. "Neural Effects of the Social Environment." *Schizophrenia Bulletin* 40 (2): 248–251.

Krieger, Nancy. 2001. "Theories for Social Epidemiology in the 21st Century: An Ecosocial Perspective." *International Journal of Epidemiology* 30 (4): 668–677.

Kubota, Jennifer T., Mahzarin R. Banaji, and Elizabeth A. Phelps. 2012. "The Neuroscience of Race." *Nature Neuroscience* 15 (7): 940–948.

Kühn, Simone, Charles Fernyhough, Benjamin Alderson-Day, and Russell T. Hurlburt. 2014. "Inner Experience in the Scanner: Can High Fidelity Apprehensions of Inner Experience Be Integrated with fMRI?" *Frontiers in Psychology* 5: 1393.

Lakoff, Andrew, Stephen J. Collier, and Paul Rabinow. 2006. "What Is a Laboratory in the Human Sciences?" Anthropology of the Contemporary Research Laboratory. http://anthropos-lab.net/wp/publications/2007/08/workingpaperno1.pdf. Accessed 3 September 2015.

Landecker, Hannah, and Aaron Panofsky. 2013. "From Social Structure to Gene Regulation, and Back: A Critical Introduction to Environmental Epigenetics for Sociology." *Annual Review of Sociology* 39 (1): 333–357.

Lane, S.N., N. Odoni, C. Landström, S.J. Whatmore, N. Ward, and S. Bradley. 2011. "Doing Flood Risk Science Differently: An Experiment

DOI: 10.1057/9781137407962.0011

in Radical Scientific Method." *Transactions of the Institute of British Geographers* 36 (1): 15–36.

Langleben, Daniel D., James W. Loughead, Warren B. Bilker, Kosha Ruparel, Anna Rose Childress, Samantha I. Busch, and Ruben C. Gur. 2005. "Telling Truth from Lie in Individual Subjects with Fast Event-Related fMRI." *Human Brain Mapping* 26 (4): 262–272.

Laplanche, Jean, and J.B. Pontalis. 1968. "Fantasy and the Origins of Sexuality." *The International Journal of Psycho-Analysis* 49 (1): 1–18.

Laplanche, Jean. 1989. *New Foundations for Psychoanalysis*. Translated by David Macey. Oxford, UK; New York, NY, USA: Basil Blackwell.

Latour, Bruno. 2012. "Paris, Invisible City: The Plasma." *City, Culture and Society* 3 (2): 91–93.

Latour, Bruno, and Steve Woolgar. 1986. *Laboratory Life: The Construction of Scientific Facts*. Reprint. Princeton, NJ: Princeton University Press.

Lederbogen, Florian, Peter Kirsch, Leila Haddad, Fabian Streit, Heiki tost, Philipp Schuch, Stefan Wüst, et al. 2011. "City Living and Urban Upbringing Affect Neural Social Stress Processing in Humans." *Nature* 474 (7352): 498–501.

Lee, Ellie, Jan Macvarish, and Pam Lowe. 2014. "The Uses and Abuses of Biology: Neuroscience, Parenting and Family Policy in Britain." http://blogs.kent.ac.uk/parentingculturestudies/files/2014/03/ UAB-Key-Findings-Report.pdf. Accessed 3 September 2015.

Lélé, Sharachchandra, and Richard B. Norgaard. 2005. "Practicing Interdisciplinarity." *BioScience* 55 (11): 967–975.

Lende, Daniel H. 2005. "Wanting and Drug Use: A Biocultural Approach to the Analysis of Addiction." *Ethos* 33 (1): 100–124.

Lende, Daniel H., and Greg Downey, eds. 2012. *The Encultured Brain: An Introduction to Neuroanthropology*. 1 edition. Cambridge, MA: The MIT Press.

Levin, Nadine. 2014. "Multivariate Statistics and the Enactment of Metabolic Complexity." *Social Studies of Science* 44 (4): 555–578.

Lewis, Glyn, and Margaret Booth. 1994. "Are Cities Bad for Your Mental Health?" *Psychological Medicine* 24 (4): 913–915.

Leys, Ruth. 2011. "The Turn to Affect: A Critique." *Critical Inquiry* 37 (3): 434–472.

Littlefield, Melissa M. 2011. *The Lying Brain: Lie Detection in Science and Science Fiction*. Ann Arbor, MI: University of Michigan Press.

Littlefield, Melissa M., Des Fitzgerald, Kasper Knudsen, James Tonks, and Martin Dietz. 2014. "Contextualizing Neuro-Collaborations:

DOI: 10.105/9781134079620.0012

Reflections on a Transdisciplinary fMRI Lie Detection Experiment." *Frontiers in Human Neuroscience* 8: 149.

Lury, Celia, Luciana Parisi, and Tiziana Terranova. 2012. "Introduction: The Becoming Topological of Culture." *Theory, Culture & Society* 29 (4–5): 3–35.

MacMynowski, Dena P. 2007. "Pausing at the Brink of Interdisciplinarity: Power and Knowledge at the Meeting of Social and Biophysical Science." *Ecology and Society* 12 (1): 20.

Mahfoud, Tara, and Sam Maclean. 2015. "Towards Neuro-Social Science: The Politics and Pragmatics of Collaboration." *Somatosphere: Science, Medicine and Anthropology*. June 10. http://somatosphere. net/2015/06/towards-neuro-social-science-the-politics-and-pragmatics-of-collaboration.html. Accessed 3 September 2015.

Margulies, Daniel S. 2011. "The Salmon of Doubt." In *Critical Neuroscience: A Handbook of the Social and Cultural Contexts of Neuroscience*, edited by Suparna Choudhury and Jan Slaby, 273–285. Chichester, W. Sussex Wiley-Blackwell.

Margulies, Daniel, Joachim Böttger, Aimi Watanabe, and Krzysztof J. Gorgolewski. 2013. "Visualizing the Human Connectome." *NeuroImage* 80 (October): 445–461.

Martin, Emily. 2004. "Talking Back to Neuro-Reductionism." In *Cultural Bodies: Ethnography and Theory*, edited by Helen Thomas and Jamilah Ahmed, 190–211. Oxford: Blackwell.

Martin, Lauren, and Anna J. Secor. 2014. "Towards a Post-Mathematical Topology." *Progress in Human Geography* 38 (3): 420–438.

Martínez Mateo, Marina, Maurice Cabanis, Nicole Cruz de Echeverría Loebell, and Sören Krach. 2012. "Concerns about Cultural Neurosciences: A Critical Analysis." *Neuroscience & Biobehavioral Reviews* 36 (1): 152–161.

Massumi, Brian. 2002. *Parables for the Virtual: Movement, Affect, Sensation*. Durham, NC: Duke University Press.

Matusall, Svenja. 2013. "Social Behavior in the 'Age of Empathy'? – A Social Scientist's Perspective on Current Trends in the Behavioral Sciences." *Frontiers in Human Neuroscience* 7: 236.

Matusall, Svenja, Ina Kaufmann, and Markus Christen. 2011. "Historical Perspectives on Social Neuroscience." In *The Oxford Handbook of Social Neuroscience*, edited by Jean Decety and John T. Cacioppo, 9–27. Oxford: Oxford University Press.

Mayer, Katja, Tomas König, and Helga Nowotny, eds. 2013. "Horizons for Social Sciences and Humanities: Workshop Report." Mykolas Romeris University Press. http://horizons.mruni.eu/wp-content/uploads/2014/02/ssh_mru_conference_report_final.pdf. Accessed 3 September 2015.

McEwen, Bruce S. 2012. "Brain on Stress: How the Social Environment Gets under the Skin." *Proceedings of the National Academy of Sciences* 109 (Suppl 2): 17180–17185.

Medical Research Council. n.d. "Skills Development Fellowships." www.mrc.ac.uk. http://www.mrc.ac.uk/skills-careers/fellowships/skills-development-fellowships. Accessed 3 September 2015.

Meloni, Maurizio. 2014a. "Biology without Biologism: Social Theory in a Postgenomic Age." *Sociology* 48 (4): 731–746.

———. 2014b. "How Biology Became Social, and What It Means for Social Theory." *The Sociological Review* 62 (3): 593–614.

Meyer-Lindenberg, Andreas, and Heike Tost. 2012. "Neural Mechanisms of Social Risk for Psychiatric Disorders." *Nature Neuroscience* 15 (5): 663–668.

Mitchell, Don. 1995. "There's No Such Thing as Culture: Towards a Reconceptualization of the Idea of Culture in Geography." *Transactions of the Institute of British Geographers*, New Series, 20 (1): 102–116.

Mol, Annemarie. 2002. *The Body Multiple: Ontology in Medical Practice.* Durham, NC: Duke University Press.

Morawski, Jill. 2007. "Scientific Selves: Discerning the Subject and the Experimenter in Experimental Psychology in the United States, 1900–1935." In *Psychology's Territories: Historical and Contemporary Perspectives from Different Disciplines*, edited by Mitchell Ash and Thomas Sturm, 129–148. Mahwah, NJ: Lawrence Erlbaum Associates.

MQ. n.d. "MQ Fellows Award." http://www.joinmq.org/research/pages/fellows-programme. Accessed 3 September 2015.

National Institute of Mental Health. 2015. "Behavioral Science and Integrative Neuroscience Research Branch." *National Institute of Mental Health.* http://www.nimh.nih.gov/about/organization/dnbbs/behavioral-science-and-integrative-neuroscience-research-branch/index.shtml. Accessed 24 July 2015.

National Science Foundation. 2015. "Interdisciplinary Behavioral and Social Science Research (IBSS)." 2015. *Interdisciplinary Behavioral*

DOI: 10.1057/9781137407962.0012

and Social Science Research (IBSS). https://www.nsf.gov/funding/
pgm_summ.jsp?pims_id=504832. Accessed 24 July 2015.

Nature. 2014. "Time for the Social Sciences." *Nature* 517 (7532): 5.

Nestler, Eric J., and Steven E. Hyman. 2010. "Animal Models of
Neuropsychiatric Disorders." *Nature Neuroscience* 13 (10): 1161–1169.

Ngai, Sianne. 2005. *Ugly Feelings*. Cambridge, MA: Harvard University
Press.

Niewöhner, Jörg. 2015. "Epigenetics: Localizing Biology through
Co-Laboration." *New Genetics and Society* 34 (2): 219–242.

Omi, Yasuhiro. 2012. "Collectivistic Individualism: Transcending a
Traditional Opposition." *Culture & Psychology* 18 (3): 403–416.

Ortega, Francisco, and Fernando Vidal. 2007. "Mapping the Cerebral
Subject in Contemporary Culture." *RECIIS: Electronic Journal of
Communication Information and Innovation in Health* 1 (2): 255–259.

Osborne, Thomas. 2013. "Inter That Discipline!" In *Interdisciplinarity:
Reconfigurations of the Social and Natural Sciences*, edited by Andrew
Barry and Georgina Born, 82–98. London: Routledge.

Oyserman, Daphna, Heather M. Coon, and Markus Kemmelmeier.
2002. "Rethinking Individualism and Collectivism: Evaluation of
Theoretical Assumptions and Meta-Analyses." *Psychological Bulletin*
128 (1): 3–72.

Panksepp, Jaak, and Mark Solms. 2011. "What Is Neuropsychoanalysis?
Clinically Relevant Studies of the Minded Brain." *Trends in Cognitive
Sciences* 16 (1): 6–8.

Papoulias, Constantina, and Felicity Callard. 2010. "Biology's Gift:
Interrogating the Turn to Affect." *Body & Society* 16 (1): 29–56.

———. 2012. "The Rehabilitation of the Drive in Neuropsychoanalysis:
From Sexuality to Self-Preservation." In *Freuds Referenzen*, edited
by Christina Kirchhoff and Gerhard Scharbert, 189–215. Berlin:
Kulturverlag Kadmos.

Pettit, Michael, Darya Serykh, and Christopher D. Green. 2015.
"Multispecies Networks: Visualizing the Psychological Research of
the Committee for Research in Problems of Sex." *Isis* 106 (1): 121–149.

Pickering, Andrew. 2013. "Ontology and Antidisciplinarity." In
Interdisciplinarity: Reconfigurations of the Social and Natural Sciences,
edited by Andrew Barry and Georgina Born, 209–225. London:
Routledge.

Pickersgill, Martyn, and Ira van Keulen, eds. 2011. *Sociological Reflections
on the Neurosciences*. Bingley, U.K.: Emerald.

DOI: 10.1057/9781137407962.0021

Pickersgill, Martyn, Jörg Niewöhner, Ruth Müller, Paul Martin, and Sarah Cunningham-Burley. 2013. "Mapping the New Molecular Landscape: Social Dimensions of Epigenetics." *New Genetics and Society* 32 (4): 429–447.

Poldrack, Russell A. 2006. "Can Cognitive Processes Be Inferred from Neuroimaging Data?" *Trends in Cognitive Sciences* 10 (2): 59–63.

Priebe, Stefan, Tom Burns, and Tom K. J. Craig. 2013. "The Future of Academic Psychiatry May Be Social." *The British Journal of Psychiatry* 202 (5): 319–320.

Pykett, Jessica. 2015. *Brain Culture: Shaping Policy through Neuroscience.* Bristol: Policy Press.

Rabinow, Paul. 2009. "Prosperity, Amelioration, Flourishing: From a Logic of Practical Judgment to Reconstruction." *Law and Literature* 21 (3): 301–320.

Rabinow, Paul, and Gaymon Bennett. 2012. *Designing Human Practices: An Experiment with Synthetic Biology.* Chicago, IL: Chicago University Press.

Raichle, Marcus E., Ann Mary MacLeod, Abraham Z. Snyder, William J. Powers, Debra A. Gusnard, and Gordon L. Shulman. 2001. "A Default Mode of Brain Function." *Proceedings of the National Academy of Sciences* 98 (2): 676–682.

Raikhel, Eugene. 2015. "From the Brain Disease Model to Ecologies of Addiction." In *Revisioning Psychiatry: Cultural Phenomenology, Critical Neuroscience, and Global Mental Health*, edited by Laurence Kirmayer, Robert Lemelson, and Constance Cummings, 375–399. Cambridge: Cambridge University Press.

Ramsden, Edmund. 2011. "Model Organisms and Model Environments: A Rodent Laboratory in Science, Medicine and Society." *Medical History* 55 (3): 365–368.

Research Councils UK. n.d. "Applications across Research Council Remits: Supporting Research Across Research Council Boundaries." http://www.rcuk.ac.uk/funding/fundingagreement. Accessed 3 September 2015.

Rheinberger, Hans-Jörg. 2010. *An Epistemology of the Concrete: Twentieth-century Histories of Life.* Durham, NC: Duke University Press.

Robson, Mary, Angela Woods, and Charles Fernyhough. 2015. "Voice Club." *Working Knowledge: Transferable Methodology for Interdisciplinary Research.* http://www.workingknowledgeps.com/wp-content/uploads/2015/03/WKPS_Voice_Club_Final.pdf Accessed 3 September 2015.

DOI: 10.1057/9781137407962.0012

Roepstorff, Andreas, and Chris Frith. 2012. "Neuroanthropology or Simply Anthropology? Going Experimental as Method, as Object of Study, and as Research Aesthetic." *Anthropological Theory* 12 (1): 101–111.

Rose, Nikolas S. 1996. *Inventing Our Selves: Psychology, Power, and Personhood.* Cambridge: Cambridge University Press.

———. 2013. "The Human Sciences in a Biological Age." *Theory, Culture & Society* 30 (1): 3–34.

———. n.d. "ENSN: European Neuroscience and Society Network. Final Report." European Science Foundation. https://www.kcl.ac.uk/sspp/departments/sshm/research/ensn/ENSN-Final-Report-January-2013.pdf. Accessed 3 September 2015.

Rose, Nikolas S., and Joelle M. Abi-Rached. 2013. *Neuro: The New Brain Sciences and the Management of the Mind.* Princeton, NJ: Princeton University Press.

Sandi, Carmen, and József Haller. 2015. "Stress and the Social Brain: Behavioural Effects and Neurobiological Mechanisms." *Nature Reviews Neuroscience* 16 (5): 290–304.

Sapolsky, Robert M. 2005. "The Influence of Social Hierarchy on Primate Health." *Science* 308 (5722): 648–652.

Sayles, Leonard R. 1976. "Matrix Management: The Structure with a Future." *Organizational Dynamics* 5 (2): 2–17.

Schaffer, Simon. 2013. "How Disciplines Look." In *Interdisciplinarity: Reconfigurations of the Social and Natural Sciences,* edited by Andrew Barry and Georgina Born, 57–81. London: Routledge.

Schmitz, Sigrid, and Grit Höppner, eds. 2014a. *Gendered Neurocultures: Feminist and Queer Perspectives on Current Brain Discourses.* Vienna: Zaglossus.

———. 2014b. "Neurofeminism and Feminist Neurosciences: A Critical Review of Contemporary Brain Research." *Frontiers in Human Neuroscience* 8: 546.

Schoenberger, Erica. 2001. "Interdisciplinarity and Social Power." *Progress in Human Geography* 25 (3): 365–382.

Seligman, Rebecca, and Ryan A. Brown. 2010. "Theory and Method at the Intersection of Anthropology and Cultural Neuroscience." *Social Cognitive and Affective Neuroscience* 5 (2–3): 130–137.

Seligman, Rebecca, and Laurence J. Kirmayer. 2008. "Dissociative Experience and Cultural Neuroscience: Narrative, Metaphor and Mechanism." *Culture, Medicine and Psychiatry* 32 (1): 31–64.

DOI: 10.1057/9781137407962.0021

Seligman, Rebecca, Suparna Choudhury, and Laurence Kirmayer. forthcoming. "Locating Culture in the Brain and in the World: From Social Categories to the Ecology of Mind." In *Handbook of Cultural Neuroscience*. New York: Oxford University Press.

Shapin, Steven, and Simon Schaffer. 1989. *Leviathan and the Air-Pump*. Princeton, NJ: Princeton University Press.

Simmel, Georg. 2002 [1903]. "The Metropolis and Mental Life." In *The Blackwell City Reader*, edited by Gary Bridge, and Sophie Watson, 11–19. Malden, MA: Blackwell.

Singh, Ilina. 2012. "Human Development, Nature and Nurture: Working beyond the Divide." *BioSocieties* 7 (3): 308–321.

Slaby, Jan, and Suparna Choudhury. 2011. "Proposal for a Critical Neuroscience." In *Critical Neuroscience: A Handbook of the Social and Cultural Contexts of Neuroscience*, edited by Suparna Choudhury and Jan Slaby, 27–51. Chichester, W. Sussex Wiley-Blackwell.

Slaby, Jan, and Shaun Gallagher. 2015. "Critical Neuroscience and Socially Extended Minds." *Theory, Culture & Society*, 32 (1): 33–59.

Smith, Tiffany Watt. 2014. *On Flinching: Theatricality and Scientific Looking from Darwin to Shell Shock*. Oxford: Oxford University Press.

Snape, K., R. C. Trembath, and G. M. Lord. 2008. "Translational Medicine and the NIHR Biomedical Research Centre Concept." *QJM: An International Journal of Medicine* 101 (11): 901–906.

Snyder, Abraham Z., and Marcus E. Raichle. 2012. "A Brief History of the Resting State: The Washington University Perspective." *NeuroImage* 62 (2): 902–910.

Solms, Mark, and Oliver H. Turnbull. 2011. "What Is Neuropsychoanalysis?" *Neuropsychoanalysis* 13 (2): 133–145.

Stavrianakis, Anthony, Gaymon Bennett, Lyle Fearnley, and Paul Rabinow. 2014. "Confusion, Truth, and Bureaucracy: A Reply to Fitzgerald and Callard." December 9. http://somatosphere. net/2014/12/confusion-truth-and-bureaucracy-a-reply-to-fitzgerald-and-callard.html. Accessed 3 September 2015.

Strathern, Marilyn, and Elena Khlinovskaya Rockhill. 2013. "Unexpected Consequences and an Unanticipated Outcome." In *Interdisciplinarity: Reconfigurations of the Social and Natural Sciences*, edited by Andrew Barry and Georgina Born, 119–140. London: Routledge.

Szerszynski, Bronislaw, and Maialen Galarraga. 2013. "Geoengineering Knowledge: Interdisciplinarity and the Shaping of Climate Engineering Research." *Environment and Planning A* 45 (12): 2817–2824.

DOI: 10.1057/9781137407962.0012

Tate. 2012. "Event Series: Topology." *Tate Modern: What's On.* http://www.tate.org.uk/whats-on/tate-modern/eventseries/topology. Accessed 3 September 2015.

Thompson, Charis. 2005. *Making Parents: The Ontological Choreography of Reproductive Technologies.* Cambridge, MA: MIT Press.

Toyokawa, Satoshi, Monica Uddin, Karestan C. Koenen, and Sandro Galea. 2012. "How Does the Social Environment 'get into the Mind'? Epigenetics at the Intersection of Social and Psychiatric Epidemiology." *Social Science & Medicine,* 74 (1): 67–74.

Varese, Filippo, Feikje Smeets, Marjan Drukker, Ritsaert Lieverse, Tineke Lataster, Wolfgang Viechtbauer, John Read, Jim van Os, and Richard P. Bentall. 2012. "Childhood Adversities Increase the Risk of Psychosis: A Meta-Analysis of Patient-Control, Prospective- and Cross-Sectional Cohort Studies." *Schizophrenia Bulletin,* 38 (4): 661–671.

Viney, William, Felicity Callard, and Angela Woods. 2015. "Critical Medical Humanities: Embracing Entanglement, Taking Risks." *Medical Humanities* 41 (1): 2–7.

VolkswagenStiftung. n.d. "European Platform for Life Sciences, Mind Sciences, and the Humanities." https://www.volkswagenstiftung.de/en/funding/completed-initiatives/european-platform.html?tx_itaofundinginitiative_itaofundinginitiativekeydates[controller]=FundingInitiative&cHash=16f8133d244d06a981e3fe74623a2daf. Accessed 3 September 2015.

Vul, Edward, Christine Harris, Piotr Winkielman, and Harold Pashler. 2009. "Puzzlingly High Correlations in fMRI Studies of Emotion, Personality, and Social Cognition." *Perspectives on Psychological Science* 4 (3): 274–290.

Wallimann, Isidor, Nicholas Tatsis, and George V. Zito. 1977. "On Max Weber's Definition of Power." *Australian and New Zealand Journal of Sociology* 13 (3): 231–235.

Waugh, Patricia. 2015. "The Novel as Therapy: Ministrations of Voice in an Age of Risk." *Journal of the British Academy* 3: 35–68.

Wellcome Trust. n.d. "Funding." http://www.wellcome.ac.uk/funding Accessed 3 September 2015.

Wilkes, James. 2015. "Weak Technology: The Voice and Body in Performance." *The Wire.* July. http://www.thewire.co.uk/in-writing/essays/weak-technology. Accessed 3 September 2015.

Wilkes, James, and Sophie Scott. forthcoming. "Poetry and Neuroscience: An Interdisciplinary Conversation." *Configurations.*

DOI: 10.1057/9781137407962.0012

Wilson, Elizabeth A. 2004. *Psychosomatic: Feminism and the Neurological Body*. Durham, NC: Duke University Press.

———. 2009. "'Would I Had Him with Me Always': Affects of Longing in Early Artificial Intelligence." *Isis* 100 (4): 839–847.

———. 2011a. "Neurological Entanglements: The Case of Paediatric Depressions, SSRIs and Suicidal Ideation." *Subjectivity* 4 (3): 277–297.

———. 2011b. "Another Neurological Scene." *History of the Present* 1 (2): 149–169.

———. 2015. *Gut Feminism*. Durham, NC: Duke University Press.

Woods, Angela. 2015. "Interdisciplinary Authorship." *Working Knowledge: Transferable Methodology for Interdisciplinary Research*. http://www.workingknowledgeps.com/wp-content/uploads/2015/02/ WK_Interd_Auth_FINAL.pdf. Accessed 3 September 2015.

Woods, Angela, Nev Jones, Ben Alderson-Day, Felicity Callard, and Charles Fernyhough. 2015. "Experiences of Hearing Voices: Analysis of a Novel Phenomenological Survey." *The Lancet Psychiatry* 2 (4): 323–331.

Woods, Angela, Nev Jones, Marco Bernini, Felicity Callard, Ben Alderson-Day, Johanna C. Badcock, Vaughan Bell, et al. 2014. "Interdisciplinary Approaches to the Phenomenology of Auditory Verbal Hallucinations." *Schizophrenia Bulletin* 40 (Suppl 4) (July): S246–S254.

Xygalatas, Dimitris, Ivana Konvalinka, Joseph Bulbulia, and Andreas Roepstorff. 2011. "Quantifying Collective Effervescence." *Communicative & Integrative Biology* 4 (6): 735–738.

Young, Allan. 2011. "Empathic Cruelty and the Origins of the Social Brain." In *Critical Neuroscience: A Handbook of the Social and Cultural Contexts of Neuroscience*, edited by Suparna Choudhury and Jan Slaby, 159–176. Chichester, W. Sussex: Wiley-Blackwell.

———. 2012. "The Social Brain and the Myth of Empathy." *Science in Context* 25 (3): 401–424.

DOI: 10.1057/9781137407962.0012

OPEN

Index

DOI: 10.1057/9781137407962.0013

DOI: 10.105/9781137407962.0013

DOI: 10.105/978113407962.0013

DOI: 10.1057/9781137407962.0013

DOI: 10.1057/9781137407962.0013

DOI: 10.1057/9781137407962.0013